BEYOND THE

Jane,

With love and
many thanks,

Piers x

BEYOND THE STILE

A Cheshire lad remembers -
hatching plots and dreaming dreams
in the countryside

Ken Wilbraham

Illustrated by JOHN TUFFNELL

ISBN
1 901253 46 5
First published November 2004

British Library Cataloguing in Publication Data.
A catalogue record for this book is
available from the British Library.

Published by
Léonie Press
13 Vale Road, Hartford,
Northwich, Cheshire CW8 1PL
Great Britain

Printed by
Anne Loader Publications
Covers laminated by The Finishing Touch, St Helens

About the author

I was born in June 1941 and my life has been dominated by science, engineering and research – firstly at home, then during my scholastic years and finally whilst employed as a Chemical Engineer by the Royal Dutch/Shell Group. I slipped comfortably into a literary straitjacket of formal, factual and precise writing. Boring, some people might say, and certainly my secondary school English teacher gave up early on my ever producing an 'imaginative' piece of writing.

Retirement in 1996 brought a determination to visit a world that had eluded me. I was now free of anyone standing over me, dictating what could or couldn't be said.

Signing up to a WEA (Workers Educational Association) course on 'creative writing' got the ball rolling. I wanted to get down on paper an account of the wonderfully carefree days spent in Guilden Sutton, a small village just outside Chester, soon after the Second World War. Progress on the page has been hindered by my passion in many other areas such as old cars, DIY, golf, sailing, gardening and taking over control of the kitchen!

Now, with some reluctance and sadness, I have arrived at the end of that journey. I hope the reader gets a fraction of the enjoyment I have had in writing it.

K Wilbraham

Contents

Acknowledgements

There is a whole shopping list of people I am indebted to, in putting together these memoirs.

Sisters Jean and Sheila and big brother Tony not only proved excellent sounding boards but of course were key actors in my childhood activities, providing cheers and tears in equal amounts.

Ted and Betty, our close neighbours, racked their brains in dredging up 'cameo' moments.

Cousin Pat and her extended family, aunts and uncles, related 'incidents' that I didn't always concur with – the truth, presumably, being somewhere in between.

Classroom action was discussed with Bob and Pete. Again we argued.

To teacher Jane and fellow WEA students for stimulating criticism, guidance and maintaining a sense of humour.

To Diane, for her literary appraisal in order that Americans may understand the dialect.

To Larry, Rick, Mike and Tony for questionable alcohol-induced suggestions.

To John Tuffnell for his efforts in producing the fine drawings.

To Sue, Tim and Clare who supported me so stoically at home, constantly asking, "will those jottings ever see light of day?"

And to many others, I thank you for your thoughts, time and encouragement.

I have tried to get as near to the truth as possible. Memory, and perhaps sensitivities, have on occasions blurred some issues. No malice is intended where people have been named. As has been said many times, I have tried not to let the truth get too much in the way of an interesting story.

Dedication

For Mum and Dad who gave me life, direction,
inspiration and love. And to little sister Jean
with whom I learnt to laugh so often in
the face of adversity.

Prologue

Trips home had become less frequent and the passing of the 'Cheshire' sign on the roadside eventually lost its once magical welcoming appeal.

Time was getting on and I felt the need for one last good look round the small rural village of Guilden Sutton, lying just to the east of Chester, where I and my siblings Tony, Sheila and Jean were born just before and during the Second World War.

Now, at the end of a long drive, I eased myself out into the country air and, armed with my camera, tried quickly to become less a stranger and more like a long-lost friend.

Energy, tension and general commotion were no longer present. There was an uncharacteristic sense of order. No more hordes of kids in their threadbare, hand-me-down clothes. No snot-festooned noses. Not a sign of a skipping rope, a soap-box truck or lads bent double playing marbles. Well-rounded women in headscarves and drab pinnies, gossiping over low garden fences, had disappeared, and been replaced by designer-clad women who loaded and unloaded their muscle-bulging new 4x4s, seemingly far too big for the tiny driveways. Oil-leaking 'bangers', two-a-penny when I lived there, were nowhere to be seen. Concrete and fancy pavers seem to be the way forward, to accommodate the ever increasing number of cars that nestle in front of the long row of semis in Guilden Sutton Lane.

I took little notice of the 'private, keep out' sign. Pushing the heavily barb-wired gate open, I began an ungainly walk across a recently ploughed field. From memory, I ticked off favourite trees that had weathered well with the passage of time. Many still stood proudly among the tidily trimmed hedges. Discovering bent rusty nails that we'd hammered in to help climbing gave me a good feeling. Perhaps I hadn't been completely forgotten. And birds overhead got me wondering whether they had managed to relax their building habits in the knowledge that they were no longer vulnerable to regular visits from gangs of lads on the lookout for eggs.

In small wooded areas that became second homes, I could still make out the whereabouts of numerous camps that we had spent many hours digging. Familiar paths that we kept open by constant use had been allowed to return to nature, making safe once more the deep traps that we dug to fend off 'visiting' gangs. And, unfortunately, many of the ponds that had given me hours of pleasure were now dry, nondescript dips in the ground.

Later that day and after much pacing up and down the streets of Chester, I figured out that the plot of land on which St Werburgh's, my Junior School, had been built, is now a small part of a very large Tesco store, squeezed in between Frodsham Street and Queen Street. That, I felt was unfair and had probably been an unequal battle for existence. The disappearance of morbid gravestones against the front wall of the school was welcome. Union Walk which ran up alongside the school and past the headmaster's room is no more. But that did little to dim the image forming in my mind as I worked my way back to Frodsham Street.

"Bend over, boy."

I couldn't help but relive the fear of that dreaded cane as it accelerated through a wide arc on its way to striking yet another backside. Perhaps the arrival of Tesco's wasn't all bad.

Heading off towards my secondary school, opposite the Town Hall, I made for a flight of steps onto the Roman Walls. Easily resisting change, they still encircle the city in a strong, comforting manner. The King's School was a maze of ancient, rambling buildings in and around Chester Cathedral. Soon after I left, it moved to a site just outside the city and a bank moved in. Heaven knows how the present incumbents manage the tight stone spiral staircases which once tested my youthful nimbleness to the limit. Struggling onto tiptoe on a bench, and peering through a small leaded-light window, I managed to look into the classroom I occupied during my first year at the school. I soon clambered down, not wanting to dwell on that part of my life too long.

I had been warned that Quaintways and Clemences were no more, but didn't want to believe it. The dance halls in Lower Northgate Street had been more important to the young people of Chester than anything else. Virtually all boy and girl relationships started there, with most finishing at the altar. Now, there are plenty of instant food places and fashion shops, but the old smooching places had gone without trace. That saddened me for a short few paces as I headed towards the centre of the city.

On foot, I was steadily regaining my bearings, but on four wheels it would have been a different matter. One-way streets, 'no entry' signs everywhere, disappearing bollards and pedestrianisation were keeping the city moving forward. Views had been opened up and familiar sites could be looked at from new angles.

Seeing the distant Welsh Hills lifted my spirits and intensified my thoughts of yesteryear. My parents had been very caring, unselfish people and had given their four children every opportunity to explore fields, woods, beaches and, more importantly, themselves.

Father wasn't too comfortable with change. My ears were again jangling to his often uttered, memorable gems:

"It's th'price thy pay for progress lad."

"But a damn eyesore all the same if you ask me."

"First it was those housing estates down village."

"And now a motorway cuttin' place in two."

"Those councillors wouldn't listen to me. Only in it for what they get out of it."

But I have rather warmed to change. Gradually and without fanfare, it has consigned to history the challenging period of rebirth that the nation had to go through after the last world war. Now, it is safely cocooned, but will never be forgotten by the youngsters that lived through those long, hard but wonderfully carefree days.

Chapter 1

The Lane

The dull red double-decker bus, spewing out black fumes from its tired-sounding engine, juddered to a halt as we approached the newly built bypass two miles east of Chester.

"Up yer get. Far as we go!" shouted the conductor unnecessarily. The handful of passengers remaining readied themselves to complete their journey home to the small hamlets of Guilden Sutton and Pipers Ash.

Leaving the driver to complete an arm-wrenching reverse manoeuvre, my friends and I raced across the dual carriageway into the long thin wood that ran up the north side of Guilden Sutton Lane. It was a wood full of vigour, with branches shooting upwards and outwards in retaliation for having been hacked down by a group of Italian prisoners of war some years earlier.

I was back where I was happiest, glad to rid myself of the strait-jacket that was the cold concrete and clay of my primary school in Chester during the late 1940s.

Wandering through, roughly heading in the direction of home, we created new tracks in the undergrowth to check the progress of birds' nests being built in bushes and up trees, looked to see if there was any interesting life in the ditches and poked our heads down holes, checking on new arrivals.

"Over here, over here. More foxes since yesterday."

If the weather was good and we were not running too late, we would dump our satchels and hang around awhile, swinging from a series of ropes that had been tied to higher branches by my big brother and his mates.

Occasionally someone would let out a great yell of excitement:

"Swans, swans overhead!"

I would shoot out of the wood, and be totally mesmerised by the sight and sound of the white giants of the airways whooshing over-head, lining up for the ponds in Latham's field on the other side of the road. Deploying their legs, raising their heads and leading edges of their wings, they glided to a perfect touchdown on the nearby water.

As the wood began to thin out, the ground dipped slightly and here, hidden from passers-by by trouser-clutching brambles, was one of our special 'gathering places'. Intimate and cosy, in the spring a carpet of blue made it even more magical. We went to great lengths to keep these covert places just that.

The narrowing of the road at this point heralded the start of a row of some forty semi-detached pebble-dashed houses erected in the 1930s as part of a Government initiative to encourage people to buy their homes, rather than rent from the Council. My parents, Charles and Helena Wilbraham, settled into number 40, about halfway along a ribbon-type development on the south side of the lane.

Who would believe that small patches of grass between the road and our front garden fences could provide so much pleasure. Apart from the makeshift tents made from our bedclothes draped over clothes horses that we erected in the summer, they acted as a series of chicanes for us to zoom up and down on our bikes and trucks made from pram wheels and wooden planks. BRM 1 was my person-alised numberplate, cut out from an old Castrol oil can. British Racing

2

Motors No.1, painstakingly painted with black enamel paint. My close mate Jack had BRM 2.

Pinched fingers, chipped teeth, grazed elbows and the occasional close examination of a solid concrete post were a small price to pay for the endless pleasure that they provided.

Later, these small parcels of grass became useful car parking areas as I graduated first to a Ford Special and then a brace of MGs, not to mention my brother's Austin 7 and my younger sister's Mini Cooper. Plus of course a multitude of visitors at weekends.

"Eh up, is that a garage you Wilbrahams are running at number 40?" quipped the neighbours regularly. But potential ill feelings were ameliorated when we were called upon to lay our skilful hands upon their troublesome vehicles. I loved problem-solving and the great adrenaline rush when everything was back in place and running smoothly. Another cuppa arrived to celebrate.

*

We had a motley group of neighbours – a postman, a railway worker, a teacher, a civil servant, a preacher, a farm labourer, an ice-cream salesman, a refinery foreman, a scrap merchant, a mechanic, a pig farmer, a fireman, an electrical engineer and the inevitable insurance salesmen – but it mattered not a jot what their parents did when forming friendships with other children. Putting behind them a bleak existence of crowded back-to-back housing in and around the Chester area was the driving force that led many of them to seek a better place to live. They were able to put some daylight between themselves and their parents for the first time in their lives. They could lay claim to having their own 'castle' in the Cheshire countryside.

My parents must have felt ten feet tall when they moved in immediately after they married. The house cost £600, paid back over 25 years to the Halifax Building Society. I can still recall the day when this burden was finally lifted from their shoulders, as they paid off the last bit with some war bonds that Father eventually recovered from a dark corner of his well-used desk.

"If you mention that sum again we'll go mental," we would scream at Father when we visited as adults many years later. Characteristic of their generation, my parents could never detach themselves from yesterday's values, had trouble with decimalisation, couldn't figure out inflation and often droned on about what you could get for half a crown just after the war.

*

"You just be careful of those Wildings. They're no-gooders," Mother would warn me.

These 'rural cowboys' lived three doors away and somehow managed to buy a strip of land that ran between the railway and the backs of our gardens. Scrap cars began to be stockpiled.

Slipping over our back fence with mates, we instantly became racing drivers as we wrenched open stiff rusty doors. While seesawing enormous plastic steering wheels, sitting on heavily padded bench seats, we pulled and twisted every knob and lever in sight. Orange semaphore arms were asking to be bent in all directions. The intoxicating aroma of a heady cocktail of resinous petrol, tired engine oil, damp carpets and mould-encrusted leather quickly had us 'brumming away' to our hearts content. And occasionally we had a fright from birds, which had set up home in glove compartments and other nooks and crannies.

Perhaps more than any other family in the neighbourhood, the Wildings had the strongest survival streak. Not afraid of physically-demanding work, their way up the social ladder was via scrap cars, a shop, building houses and eventually running various forms of 'night-time' entertainment in Chester. Too much time in the classroom would have hindered their progress to such riches.

*

Good old enterprising Mr Bates.

He cleverly converted an antiquated black Rolls-Royce into a mobile 'variety store.' I heard from the grapevine it had been a hearse first time round.

In funereal style he would trundle slowly past on his weekly visit to the lane, supplying mainly those things that hard-working house-wives were likely to run out of before another excursion to far-off Chester could be thought about. Mother would always complain about his prices. Father, if around, would proffer caution.

"Mind how much you pay, Nell. Man's a crook."

"Well how about you goin' to Hoole, Charlie, on bike if you think you can save a bit," Mother would occasionally weakly utter back, not bothering whether Father heard or not.

Mr Bates sold cabbages, wooden clothes pegs, Bachelor's peas, Gumption paste cleaner, Oxo cubes, Wren's shoe polish and other essential commodities.

We had to rely on the state of the labels wrapped round the tins to hazard a guess as to how long they had been hanging around on his rickety wooden shelving. I recall corned beef tasting very appetising twenty or more years after leaving the shores of Argentina. We never had food poisoning and a sell-by date would have been an irrelevance because we had to eat anything and everything that came into the house.

Sensing a business opportunity, the one-armed pint-size matriarch of the Wilding clan set up her general store in a converted house in competition. That she could handle the dangerous looking shiny red bacon slicing machine with such aplomb fascinated me on my rare visits.

Mother was always pleased to see the fresh fish man turn up on a Friday. It eased her Catholic conscience.

"Mum, can't we have fish and chips from the 'chippie' in Cedar Grove, like our friends?"

Every week the same plaintive plea was uttered by one of the four of us, and every week she replied that her fresh fish was better for us. Just occasionally, maybe on a birthday or a Holy Day, we were allowed to cross the bypass to get stuck into some real fish and chips, snugly wrapped in old copies of the *Cheshire Observer*.

There were other regulars that trailed their wares along the lane. You could set your clock daily to Mr Frodsham's horse-drawn milk float. As he ladled out of his churn into Mother's jug, his horse, having struggled all the way from Mickle Trafford a mile or more away, would often take advantage of the stop and leave a steaming brown hillock which always amused me and my little sister but which disgusted my elder sister.

"Don't be so silly, you two. Grow up. It's only natural."

So much for big sisters. Big brother was too embarrassed to say anything.

Meanwhile, Father on hearing the news, or rather smelling it, was hot-foot down the path, shovel in hand to claim his prize.

"It's outside our house. It's ours."

Some would be spread on his rhubarb and some set aside for the roses he threatened to get one day. He was always happy having something for nothing.

Scrap dealer Patsy Dobbins was a weekly touter and one day took away our well-used favourite rocking horse. It had seen better days and Mother gave the nod so that she had a bit more space to get nearer to her washing line in the overcrowded back yard.

Father, quite simply had an apoplectic fit when he came home from work and was never the same man again. Mother had temporarily 'forgotten the world' according to Father.

"Never throw anything out lad, 'cos one day t'will come in useful!"

The heroics of the pedalling ice-cream man took some beating. Only on a Sunday were we allowed to approach his heavy, cumbersome-looking trike, parked on the kerbside. We took it in turn to ask for a "a pink and white block please".

With the dinner plates sided away, it would make its royal entrance onto the table from our miniscule fridge. Father would ready his 12-inch steel rule for the cutting operation to head off any possibility of squabbling amongst my siblings. None of us wanted the end bits. They tended to melt and short-change the unlucky recipient.

"Have you washed up lately or cleaned your bedrooms?" Father would ask somewhat forlornly, trying to get a feel whether any favouritism was in order. How could he possibly discriminate between his four nigh-perfect children?

A trail of dust in the air heralded the presence of Mr Cobden the coalman. Not only was his coal vital but the hessian sacks were in great demand. Well-washed and stitched together, they made rag carpets which surprisingly were more cosy than you might imagine.

"But don't tell me boss 'bout sacks, cos he'll wring me neck," bellowed the leather-clad delivery lad, disappearing down the path like an armadillo after he'd dumped the final load 'round back of t'house'.

*

"Hello, Mr and Mrs Dare, how are Ethel, John, Jill, Sandra, Deryck, Elaine, Norman, Clifford…" and so on 'til all eleven names had been rattled out. It was the normal banter among the cheekier lads on meeting them.

And they weren't even Catholics.

The row of quaint, old cottages in Heathbank where they lived, leaking smoke incessantly from squat chimneys, began where our relatively fancy new pebble-dashed houses ended, stopping just short of a bridge that took the lane over the railway buried in a deep cutting. They were classic 'two-up, two-down' dwellings, and cold water had to be drawn from a pump in Lindop's, their neighbour's front garden. Not surprisingly poor Mrs Dare always looked 'down on her uppers' and her husband seemed to have little energy left to do anything other than his siring duties.

I was friendly with John, one of the older boys, and his lack of material wealth was never an issue when we entered our world of play. On the contrary, he attracted our respect in getting on with life whilst being well below the breadline most of the time. They operated a sort of shift system in order to grab sleep in somewhat cramped conditions, but we never probed too closely on that potentially embarrassing subject. I often wonder how life panned out for them. I heard more moans and complaints from an only child than all the Dares' kids put together.

On the far side of the bridge, wizened Mrs Anderton maintained her familiar stooped position in the garden well into old age. Her extensive rhubarb patch, spilling out onto the railway 'batters', joined forces with red campion, primroses and cowslips. It resembled a collection of umbrellas blown inside out and was by far the biggest in the neighbourhood. I swear some of the sticks weighed more than she did. They were certainly thicker than her legs. Mixed with lemon jelly, rhubarb became one of our favourite puddings.

"Must be smoke from the trains," some budding 'Percy Thrower' in my family would regularly comment.

I often saw Mr Anderton throwing papers and parcels to his wife from the guard's van as the train he was working passed by on its last journey of the day.

"Saves me t'effort carrying it back from Chester General Station on bike," he would shout to us nosy kids as we leant inquisitively over the bridge parapet, our heads deeply buried in the swirling gritty grey smoke rising around us.

Opposite Anderton's cottage, a Council dump set well back from the road quietly absorbed rubbish brought in on lorries. Not that there was a great deal and there would have been even less if Father's hoarding instincts had been contagious. String, wood, boxes, bits of metal, bottle tops — they all warranted close inspection by Father as he cycled past. Later, in the comfort of his Ford Consul with mandatory roof-rack, his stock grew more rapidly.

A stone's throw further on, a comforting, clucking sound could always be heard coming from Evans' chicken farm. All the family enjoyed visits there, collecting eggs from genuinely free-range hens left to their own devices in a large orchard — hens that diligently scrubbed around in the earth for beetles, grubs, worms, spiders, swill and the like. They produced enormous brown eggs that often contained 'double-yolkers' — deep yellow like the setting sun and extremely yummy. We fought over the biggest at the dinner table and never for one moment thought about the hens' diet!

The mother of one of my mates rationed him and his siblings to only half an egg each at meal time. Money was a struggle in many families.

If we managed to get our parents in the right frame of mind, we occasionally left with cardboard boxes under our arms containing day-old chicks, breathing though holes that we'd hurriedly punctured in the sides with sheath knives.

The lane swept eastwards, easing itself slightly downwards, curving one way then the other, appearing to narrow as the tall unkempt hawthorn hedgerows hemmed it in, past the track to Dandy's farm on the left, our potato supplier. Calamity struck here one day when the shopping bag got caught in the front wheel of my bike. Head down I was going full tilt. Then the road was a sea of spuds and blood was pouring from my arms, legs and head. There was no escape from the close scrutiny of the audience that always seemed to be on hand when adversity struck. The buckled front wheel was well and truly jammed. Sad to say my body and bike recovered more quickly than my pride.

Isolated cottages then began popping up here and there out of the surrounding fields, before the village school and the Square came into view. The road now descended Porters Hill, pouring itself into the welcoming arms of the heart of the village, cosily sitting in a large flat bowl that nature had sculpted out of the surrounding land. A T-junction marked the symbolic heart of the village, being grandly endorsed by a war memorial and nineteenth century Methodist church looking sternly down as you eased to a halt.

*

"Eh up, lad. That's rubbish. You haven't bin round long enough to know."

My dad would often pontificate, while sitting by the dozing coke fire in pensive mood, listening to the crackling radio, which he said he would fix one day but never did. His NHS-issued specs, much repaired by tape and glue, perched on the end of his Mr Punch nose and a newspaper always languished across his knees. He must have felt bare without it. Platefuls of dripping toast completed the scene.

"Too damned airy-fairy a reason if you ask me," he muttered.

The fact that William the Conqueror saw fit to include Guilden Sutton in the Domesday Book, referring to it as "the southern homestead in the hollow where the marsh marigolds grow," didn't convince Father as to its origin.

"Listen. The village got its name from a load of gold buried by Royalists fleeing for their lives when Oliver Cromwell's men hit town."

Father's encyclopaedia mania, as normal, began kicking in.

"And it's never bin found since. So get out there with your shovels, you kids."

God, my father impressed me. He could move effortlessly from explaining electrical hysteresis to medieval history at the drop of his tatty brown trilby.

Like all dads, he was never wrong. Well, not until I was about ten.

*

With war well and truly buried, I witnessed farmers in the village being frog-marched into the future. Long gone were the blacksmiths, the brick and boot makers. The arrival of piped water and gas had helped breathe extra life into the place.

Diesel-guzzling Fordson Major tractors began to make an appearance on distant skylines. Muscles bulging, they made light of the terrain, pulling the first combine harvesters and crop sprayers in the area.

Milking parlours arrived, mimicking man's teat-tugging exertions.

Farm labourers were disappearing by the cart load.

Faster trains and bigger lorries whisked more stuff in and then whisked more stuff out again.

But one place resisted all change. Our Local: The Bird in Hand.

Apart, that is, from landlords, who came and went.

It has remained a bastion of the past, and discreetly hidden in the village, it has served the community well for over 400 years.

Once, dishevelled hirsute haymakers straight out of the fields could be seen rubbing shoulders with clandestine couples conducting illicit affairs.

Today I doubt whether 'things' have changed all that much.

Well, maybe less of the former and more of the latter.

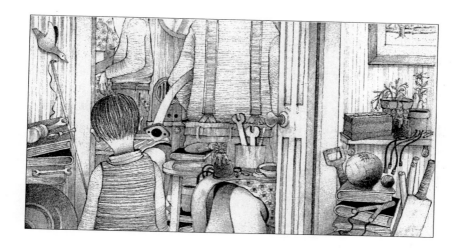

Chapter 2

Anything went at Number 40

"Dad, why Rosedale? Why choose a fancy name?"

"Your mother's idea when we first moved in."

"But where are the roses? And shouldn't you have a name somewhere to help the postman? You tell everyone we live at Rosedale."

"Don't worry lad, I'll get round to putting a sign up one day."

He even went and got headed paper sporting the name.

The sign never did appear.

And neither did the roses.

Goings and comings were only a little less frenetic than at the slightly more famous Number 10 down south. Mind you, we were a little thin on the ground with celebrities and really famous people. Not even a local councillor or a policeman ever crossed our doorstep.

Was it a home?

A garage?

A workshop?

It was all these and more, depending on who you were and what you wanted.

"And blimey, that place of yours, Ken. Always sommat' goin' on there."

It was a homely mix of nature and nurture that signed the four of us up for life.

The route to my future was being laid thoughtfully and thoroughly by my parents in their three-bedroom, pebble-dashed semi.

Father's pursuit of knowledge and Mother's innate artistic ability were the catalysts that propelled us into so many areas of interest. We got a regular dose of advice.

"Waste not, want not."

"Every job, two hands."

"Look at it logically, lad. Use your gumption."

"Don't cut corners."

"Things don't grow on trees, don't you know."

"No lad. Hold it like this, not like that."

"And prepare job properly, not like the eyesores that bloke next door gets up to."

Would I be rich if I got a penny for every time Father uttered these bits of advice! But they did pay rich dividends as we set out on our adult lives. Out of such simplicity came a confident, self-dependency approach to life. It gave us a secure and strong base from which we approached all sorts of problems. No job ever appeared too big to tackle once broken down into smaller parts. And we rarely had to go out to the shops to buy anything.

What Father was saying to his flock was, "If you put your mind to doing something, think about it carefully. Measure up properly and do it with what you have that is readily available.

"And you will succeed!"

Just as important, we had to be prepared to accept criticism. Believe me, it came in barrowfuls, particularly if Father knew that corners had indeed been cut. Interestingly, praise was hard to come by. A plausible explanation is that being a perfectionist, he never wanted you to think for one moment that you had 'cracked it,' that you could sit back on your laurels, that there was nothing more to do. So whilst encouragement was always present, we got into a thinking process that there were always improvements to be had with any job.

Mother, also, wasn't exempt from Father's helpful comments. Domestic equilibrium was achieved when we all teamed up against Father but we could never pin him down to accept he was less than 100 per cent right all the time.

*

Making sure we did our corrections on schoolwork was more important to him than eating or probably going to church.

"It's the only way to learn, son." He must have despaired of me a million times. He was in love with learning. His enormous collection of books resided everywhere, from toilet to attic, via the stairs and landing. I can't ever recall him not coming up with the information anyone needed on any subject. Occasionally you had to be patient as he was side-tracked by other interesting subjects he was boning up on.

Mother's contribution was more low-key but nevertheless just as profound. Encouraging sounds and comforting words were two of her hallmarks. She ran a free house for inmates and visitors alike. Little attempt was made to mimic an ideal home and she often harped on about relatives who ran their houses like palaces with everything in place. You know the type. Made their children go through a sort of sheep dip, back and front. A bit more grime at Number 40 was lost amongst the myriad books strewn around the place and the countless mechanical bits and pieces that found sanctuary in the dust-laden corners of rooms.

Flat surfaces. That's what we all needed plenty of. Couldn't get enough. In the summer months we tried to keep a bit out of Mother's way and stick to the garage and the lean-to that grew in size, year by year, at the back of the house.

But come bad weather, how d'you expect a budding racing car mechanic to operate with the risk of frostbite? Even the battered, heroic Valor stove couldn't fend off the penetrating northerly winds that easily ripped through the great array of gaps. So dark nights and plummeting temperatures plunged us into hibernation mode. Wheel bearings, bike brakes, dynamos and the like cosied up to text books and plates of food on the kitchen table and in the dining room.

But not the front room. Oh no, not the front room. It was not a lounge but a front room. Only posh people had lounges. It was sacrosanct and only for visitors on a Sunday. The rest of the week it was out of bounds. Mother did make a token gesture to provide a haven where respectably dressed visitors could sit down in the knowledge that their finery wouldn't come in contact with dripping oil, or big brother's vast array of chemicals and formalin-preserved snakes in bottles. And for that matter from Father's vast array of evil-looking brews made from just about everything that grew in the hedgerows around.

*

If only Mother's old gas cooker, residing in the back kitchen, could have spoken its mind, or answered back!

"Won't be a minute Mum..."

"Your minutes are never ending, m'lad."

The shiny, grey fuming liquid lead had been simmering away for some time. I'd had a bit of trouble making a clean impression of a toy soldier in the sand. Now I was ready to pour.

"You're stopping Mother making lunch," piped up my little sister, Jean. "Get a move on! And anyway, you've got enough lead soldiers already to sink a ship,"

"Want a hand?"

"No thanks Tony, I've two already."

Big brother quickly got out the way as I picked up the pan and dropped it even quicker, having got hold of the wrong bit in a panic.

"Get out of my way, you lot. I was all right 'til you came."

Some of the lead spilt out across the cooker top but there was still enough to pour into the mould. Job completed, I took my bits into the lean-to and impatiently wriggled the still hot, but now solid, soldier free of the sand. Fantastic. Just wait till I show my mate Jack. He'll be impressed.

Father was always itching to get his infernal glue pot back on the boil.

"Got to get door frame back together, Nell. Wind beginning to kick up. And you'll only complain if I don't keep t'elements out."

"That can wait awhile, Charlie. I've more important things to do. Like cook a meal for you lot."

Later, Father plumbed in a Bunsen burner to one side of the stove. Balanced precariously on a rusty old tripod stand, his smelly glue pot was now on perpetual display.

*

"Toffee! Toffee, children. Who'd like to help?"

Hardly had the words left Mother's mouth, than there was a good-size gathering of kids draped round her battle-scarred pinny. Impatient dirty little hands would quickly infiltrate, delving in, doing this, doing that. Supposedly helping. And repeated requests for tasting to check progress. If we'd had a rare windfall that week, treacle and nuts might also be added to the sugar and butter. Arguments were quickly quelled by the mouth-watering smell that began to circulate in the air. Cooled and cracked into jagged golden pieces, the shelf life of the toffee was measured in seconds.

Mother, having worked in the bakery business before marriage, had little time for written-down recipes. They had all been logged away in her head from years of practice.

"*Feel*, that's what it was all about," she reminded us time and again.

And by being allowed to work alongside her, my siblings and I quickly inherited this skill. Using small, medium and large handfuls was just as good and quicker than working slavishly from recipes to the nearest ounce. And far less washing-up.

*

Autumn time dramatically increased the load on our cooker.

"Charlie, the Kilner jars. Where are they? Hope you haven't been

15

using them in your garage again for paint. Or using them to pee in."

Invariably most of them were tracked down, lurking in a cardboard box stowed deeply in a sunken cupboard under the stairs, squeezed up against an enormous earthenware pot full of eggs, quietly minding their own business in waterglass solution.

For weeks, Mother's grand-looking copper skillet hardly took a rest.

Sugar, sugar, sugar,

Plums, apples, pears, rhubarb, strawberries, raspberries, blackcurrants, blackberries,

Peel, peel, peel,

Core, core, core,

Stir, stir, stir,

Bubble, bubble, bubble,

Pickles, onions, chutney,

Bubble, bubble, bubble,

Test, test, test,

Hot jars, hot jars, hot jars,

Wax paper, elastic bands, rubber seals,

Tops, tops, tops.

We didn't bother with labels.

It must have given my parents a good feeling to see kitchen shelves steadily filling up once again. We were ready to face another winter.

Tradition dies hard in my family and this seasonal potting activity is still alive and well; all of us regularly using such goodies as passports when we visit one another.

Our faithful cooker still had one or two other tricks in its repertoire. Plunging her curling tongs into the flames for a few seconds, a wipe on a bit of the local newspaper, Mother then set about rejuvenating her hair by a twist here and a twist there. It was quick and infinitely cheaper than a perm – even though it left a terrible pong in the kitchen.

Enterprising big brother, always knocking on the door of the impossible, made pots from clay dug up in the back garden. They entered the oven as pieces of beauty, to emerge an hour or two later as a pile of rubble. Time and time again. A rare failure for him and one that the rest of the family laughed about for a long time.

*

Father's ability to collect anything and everything was legendary. Part of this practice no doubt stemmed from the period in which my parents lived. Having their children around the time of the Second World War might be interpreted as not being too smart a move. It must have posed enormous problems in bringing up four youngsters and no doubt sharpened my parents' survival instincts to the point that they could see some intrinsic value in anything from a cardboard box to a scrap piece of wood lying by the roadside.

So year after year, his 'stock' as he euphemistically called it, grew and grew. So did the reputation of Number 40.

"That Charlie Wilbraham, he'll be able to fix it for you," became a common cry down the lane.

Bikes, trucks and prams would be brought back from the dead, with the careful attention of my father working in his large garage-cum-workshop.

Electrical work was a particular favourite of his and I can still visualise dozens of electric motors strewn across the oil stained, heavily gnarled benches, with solenoids, carbon brushes and rotors in various states of disrepair.

The occasional motor saw some life again. In reality, and this only occurred to me many years later, the main reason for collecting and investigating many of the machines was the challenge of finding out what had gone wrong or where they had failed, with little or no attempt being made to put them together again. Well, only occasionally.

We went through the inevitable apprentice stage, graduating steadily, and sometimes impatiently, to the more exciting challenges.

Soon our mates realised 'those Wilbrahams will sort it,' and they started arriving with their bits and pieces. From bikes we moved on to scooters, motorbikes and finally cars.

With a hoisting system, lathe and a wide range of tools we were ready to tackle most jobs.

Father built a pit in the garage to work underneath vehicles. As usual, it was never quite finished, and lack of waterproofing meant that a major baling-out operation was required each time. Strangely it always fell to me, being the youngest male.

The prospect of meeting several toads that had made it their temporary home was not something I looked forward to.

*

Ted Littler, a neighbour at Number 36 and lifelong friend of Tony, was constantly coming round to 'see some of the action'.

"Woch yer up to now, Wibby?" he would shout coming through the gate.

"Hi Ted, just a simple project. Making a TV out of an old box, some string, and a pot of glue," replied my brother.

Somewhat apocryphal, but those that had entered the inner sanctum of Number 40 will get the message.

Another lingering memory is knowing the make of car Father drove from the profile generated by the stock as he parked it in the garage. Simultaneously, tyres, bumper, grill, bonnet, windscreen and roof rack all made contact during the final parking manoeuvre. Any smart comments by his family as to the amount of rubbish in the way, was met by "you know where to come when you want something!"

Alas, a lot of stock requires a lot of control. If there was one thing that Number 40 lacked, it was just that. Although Father always gave the impression that he knew exactly what he had in the garage, it was an entirely different matter in actually tracking it down when needed. Invariably the desired object came to light, months and sometimes years after the initial search. And that always pleased him, even though the 'customer' might well have passed on in the meantime.

We were all so excited as the studio at the rear of the garage was nearing completion. Constructed by Father out of waste wood, old window frames and bits of roofing felt gathered over the years,

Mother was looking forward to setting up her easel and beginning to paint again. Something she last did at school. Sadly, however, Father beat her to it, filling it with great quantities of wood, fit only for the fire, that had been languishing for decades against the wall at the top of the garden. It was promises all the way with Father, saying that it was only a temporary home.

As with many other things at Number 40, 'temporary' solutions very soon became 'permanent' ones.

Chapter 3

Enjoyment through enterprise

"They can wait till the end of the over," we all muttered to ourselves.

Jack bowled his eighth and final ball.

"OK, get the stumps up. Make way for 'em."

We slouched to the side of the road, scooping up the wooden blocks holding the cricket stumps. The patiently waiting traffic trundled back into motion, almost with an apologetic air, having disrupted our game. Not even the dark green market day special single-decker Crosville bus, a sort of umbilical cord that ran the farming community from the village into Chester once a week was exempt.

"No, you can have the next over but one."

"It's Pete's turn next. Richard, you can wait ages 'cos you've only just come off."

"And Johnny, you haven't got 45. Only 44 because it wasn't a proper boundary that last shot."

Such cross-fire arguments inevitably broke out. A quick kangaroo court, set up by the boastful farming Parker boys and the roughneck Wildings, passed judgment and the game was on again. We wanted action, not discussion.

Easter was the wake-up call that galvanised us into action for the cricket season. Lads went off to ransack their dads' sheds for linseed oil and the air positively reeked of the golden nectar as we lovingly rubbed it into the bat's face with torn-up old flannelette cloth. That is, for the few of us that were lucky enough to have a proper bat.

"No wonder I can't find anything when I want it," bellowed my father as he poked his head into my bedroom, attracted by the smell.

"And don't waste it and there'd better be enough left when I want to make some putty, because that's what I bought it for."

"What on earth are you doing with that cardboard?" my sisters Sheila and Jean would scoff, knowing perfectly well what I was doing with it. Stuffed down the front of my socks, it protected my shins. It served its purpose until Father had another good day at a church jumble sale, riding up the path with a pair of real cricket pads strapped to his crossbar. Like most things arriving at our house, they had seen 'better days'. But what the heck. They were the business. Scrubbed and whitened, I went to bed that night dreaming about opening for England next day against the visiting West Indies.

The better and keener you thought you were, the nearer the bat you stood, and tall lads tucked themselves up against the garden fences to save boundaries. The fields, on the other side of a deep ditch and hawthorn hedge were patrolled by the not so serious, unprotesting types and the occasional brave girl that plucked up courage to play. They often sloped off home when they became bored without anyone noticing. I couldn't blame them for they never bowled and rarely saw the bat.

We all brushed aside twisted ankles, sprained wrists and bruises for fear of being labelled weaklings. Those less keen on cricket, but not wanting to dip out on the social interplay, shinned up a nearby oak tree and spectated. Wedged in the branches at obscure angles their legs dangled down in mid air.

"Ted! Hey Ted, did you see it from up there? He was out, wasn't he?"

"Wot? Heck, dunno Ken, was reading me book."

"And whistling tunelessly," I added to myself.

"Thanks Ted, thanks for nothin'."

If the weight of opinion was not clear one way or the other, it was 'Three bat handles from half way.' That normally sent the batsman packing. Proceedings often came to an end when the ball had been slogged into an inhospitable wooded area.

"See ya. Tarraa."

"Me dad wants me."

"Late for me dinner already."

"Got me homework to finish."

"Yer, yer," I thought. "Same people with same excuses."

Only my close mates helped to search for the ball. And lo and behold, when the vital component was once again to hand, front doors opened, important chores having miraculously finished in double quick time.

Certain gardens were definitely no-go areas. Number 34 spelt disaster. Old man Croftie's house. Always, always, this rather forlorn-looking postman had a fag drooping from his lower lip. He was a serious chain smoker at over eighty-a-day Capstan Full Strength.

When not doing his deliveries he divided his time between fishing and his garden. He lived for his garden, forever tending, tying and trimming.

He grew the biggest and proudest delphiniums in the lane, until we scythed them down from time to time with errant shots. It mattered not who hit it. The ball owner got it in the neck. I regularly received the sharp edge of his tongue and he never held back on his limited repertoire of four-letter words. He sensibly delivered his sermon from the safety of his garden, for Mr Croft was little more than skin and bone.

And for some strange reason he constantly reminded us:

"Me lads John and Michael have handles to their names, so you lot use 'em."

Somehow his sons, to keep in our good books, would drip-feed their father's ball collection back into circulation from time to time.

*

"Duck, Charlie!"

"Hey up, wot th'hell was that?"

A dull thud signalled a fast moving cricket ball striking the front wall of Number 40 between the bay window and front door.

My dad scrambled back to his knees, where he was laying yet another concrete path with the loose gravel he regularly collected from the roadside.

"By gum, Nell, doesn't bear thinking about if that had bin a couple of inches lower."

We didn't have to grovel to get the ball back. Mind you they let us know their feelings as they slung the offending object back over the drunken chestnut paling fencing.

"I wish you'd give over doing that."

With our house doubling as a sort of pavilion where most of the kit came from, there was a certain inevitability that the pitch should be right outside. It mattered little for my parents. Their garden wasn't quite a concrete jungle for we proudly displayed a deep red peony bush, which my sisters used for making their version of Chanel scent from the petals.

And a lilac tree.

"It's the double type, don't you know," Mother would often add.

It was a tough old tree for it had to fight for space with trucks, prams, bikes and bits of cars. And also fight against Father, eyeing up another part of his estate that he felt needed a concrete makeover. Every year it reminded me that life still existed in its battered branches as it burst into colour soon after Easter.

As the sun rose higher in the sky and evenings stretched out beckoning summer, other activities started to capture our imagination.

"Blimey, Kenneth, that stuff really pongs. I can't do my homework properly. Go outside to put it on."

Such an outburst from my sisters heralded the onset of some serious running.

"It's only wintergreen. You're out of your mind," I retorted.

The gnarled, loose fitting cork could hardly keep at bay the penetrating odour of the embrocation lurking in the round, wickerwork-clad stone bottle. Without it, my pulled muscles took ages to recover. A good old fashioned rub-down and I was back in action, double-quick time.

Mind you, there was a bit of controversy surrounding the Parker boys from next door. Our main training area was what we grandly named the 'Belle Vue Circuit', a series of country lanes that encircled a roughly rectangular area, judged to be exactly two miles round for time-keeping and record purposes. Cheating wasn't normally on the agenda those days. Or was it?

"Look at Tony Parker's time!" shrieked one of the keener runners.

"It's not possible. Must have cheated."

"Yer, must have done," muttered someone else.

Stout, unfriendly wire-netting, frolicsome bullocks and vigilant farmers posed a bit of a challenge for those looking for short cuts.

"That's it then," said 'Kellogg' Paddy with a prominent Adam's apple, our resident Sherlock Holmes.

"The farmers. His dad knows them all. Short cut job, I reckon," was his interpretation of the situation. It was probably a fair assessment and another crisis was quickly wrapped up.

Come the highlight of our athletics calendar at the Summer Fete down at 'Duttons The Byatts' farm, the Parker boys didn't get a look in, apart from the occasional win in the sack and egg 'n spoon races.

Boy, that pleased everyone not called Parker.

*

Occasionally, on a Saturday afternoon, and not needed by my

father to dig or break up bricks, I would bike down with my mates to the village to see the bigger lads playing football in the district league.

The ever-generous Farmer Dutton again gave over a field for this activity.

But what a field! It looked more like a lunar landscape on arrival.

I would go early to witness the hilarious preparation ritual.

"Have enough lads arrived yet?" spluttered the skipper through a haze of smoke, getting down from his tractor.

"Right. Cow pats first. Flatten 'em all out 'cos ref won't let match start. We can't let the oppo' see the pitch looking like this."

There was no attempt to cut the lush, long grass. That was very much controlled by the appetite of the cows in the previous week. Lime from the nearest builder's pit was appropriated for lining work to start.

The visiting teams rarely mastered the undulating contours. After all, a one-in-10 slope does take some getting used to.

"Is this where we're changing?" enquired newcomers to the countryside.

"Yep, that barn over there. The chickens won't peck and just shoo out the cows if they get too inquisitive," added our goalie.

Talk about home advantage. Most of the village players lived and breathed in and around the fields. Impressive wins, often going into double figures were regularly chalked up. When the action stopped, mud-splattered torsos were sluiced down in an old cast iron bath in the corner of the field, given up temporarily by the horses whilst the footballers were around. Thank goodness the country had a relaxed attitude to risk-taking in the 1950s. The local practices of Guilden Sutton FC would not have gone down too well with today's 'Health and Safety Executive'.

*

"Leave us be. Go away. We don't spoil your games. Beetle off."

The whirling of skipping ropes only attracted us lads if we had nothing better to do. Up and down the lane, earnest-looking red-faced girls churned their ropes with brightly coloured wooden handles. They hung around, executed fancy crossed hands and 'bump' movements tirelessly, stopping only to retie their hair or recover drooping knickers from around their knees.

"Stop it, you're wearing it away and my father has only just laid it."

Another bossy outburst by my eldest sister, having a go at Betty Littler of Number 36 as she skipped at the front of our new concrete driveway. I don't suppose she could help the superior air she adopted. The nuns at the Ursuline Convent in Chester were responsible for that.

This was warm-up time for the girls. Most of them wanted to see the appearance of the longer rope, heralding the formation of teams, exciting chatter and an opportunity to work on friendships. Even lads occasionally squeezed into the line, working their way down the rope as it was wound round faster and faster.

Proceedings often ended when an irate mother clutching an armful of nappies and shirts appeared on the doorstep demanding her washing line back. My sisters would disappear with their friends to play 'two ballie' or handstands against the nearest wall whilst I went back with my mates to whatever brain-numbing activity I was involved in before.

Gender differences were buried for the popular catch-all games – spur of the moment activities that got the competitive element fired up in next to no time. I often wondered who on earth had dreamt up the game of hopscotch. A small stone, bit of chalk and a flat piece of ground – that's all we needed to test our mental and physical agility to the limit. Throwing, counting, stretching, jumping on one leg and spinning in double quick time. And also have a plausible list of excuses ready when you cocked things up for your team!

Our version of 'hide and seek' was a free-for-all. We always seemed to cajole an uncomplaining type, a soft touch, to kick off with and by the time they'd counted to fifty, most of us has disappeared deep into the woods, gallivanting off across fields, up trees or into garden sheds. We had no intention of returning and often formed up in small groups to play some other game. We were so 'orrible to the person that was 'on'.

French cricket, rounders and 'tick' were some of the other games that I played and had wide appeal, irrespective of age or sex. They were games in which we all stood a chance of some glory, even if it was only fleetingly. The more the merrier seemed to be the maxim for success.

*

Our graduation to two wheels from a kid's trike was a scary experience. There was no halfway house. It had to be an adult machine. And not just an adult one but a male version with a crossbar. Did that bit of steel tubing cause us trouble, not to mention bruising to rather tender parts of our anatomy. So desperate were we to ride 'grown up' bikes, we set about necessary modifications. Immediately the seat had to be lowered as much as possible and big wooden blocks bolted onto the pedals. Even so, for the smaller kids this was still not enough. So they had to ride by placing one leg through the frame below the crossbar in order to pedal. To passers-by we must have looked like a circus troupe going through a practice routine. The dangers were only too apparent when we smiled – chipped and missing teeth were the order of the day.

The next move in 'customising' our bikes was to fit strips of thick cardboard or flexible metal to the frame, poking into the rear wheel. The faster we went the greater the sound resembled a motorbike and must have driven our mothers mental. And to compound parental tensions, we raided the cutlery drawer for forks which doubled up as tyre levers when mending a puncture. They always got them back but it looked as if Uri Geller had paid a visit.

*

"Hey Jack, just got some new glass ollies from Woollies. Got fantastic swirly colours in them. Fancy a game?"

"I'll be back in a mo," he replied, sprinting home at breakneck speed to get his hallowed treasures. We kept our marbles securely in white linen bags that once housed flour. I tended to play with close mates so that I could win back any favourites that I had lost in the regular contests we had. Some of the more memorable battles were conducted in the gutters bordering the roads round about. Looking more like a couple of hunchbacks from Notre Dame, we often covered mile after mile locked in deadly battle.

Believe it or not but milk bottles had appeal and in the winter, Jack Frost magically made ice lollies appear out of their glass necks. Perched on top were cardboard discs which gave way to silver foil in the Fifties. But I was only interested in the disc covers. Vital equipment to play a really exciting game called – 'milk bottle tops'! Doesn't sound too exciting. But it was my favourite one-to-one game for a year or two, requiring great skill at flicking discs to topple another one propped up at the base of a wall, with the winner taking all those discs that had been flicked.

I built up a huge collection. Thousands. Well, hundreds. Maybe dozens. The Co-op was the largest supplier of milk down the lane and apart from attempting to keep hungry birds at bay, the discs were a natural advertising hoarding, albeit a small one, with such memorable slogans as,

'Co-Op coal: grate stuff this!'
'Coffee and cocoa made with our milk is delicious.'
'Drink more milk and be fit.'
'Co-Op Boots and Shoes for style and comfort.'
'Milk enriches life.'

They were good clean campaigns with no whiff of hanky-panky. That was 1950 for you.

Chapter 4

Herding instincts

We were inseparable, Dave and Jack and me. Forever going round on our trucks and bikes, walking the fields, sharing secrets and when it was raining we played in one another's homes as if they were our own. Likewise, most of the other lads and girls in the lane had close buddies to share their secrets with.

But for many activities small intimate groups were not enough. Larger groups formed in a random fashion as and when necessary, their structure and content varying according to what was on offer – cricket, football, fishing, swimming, trucking, nature walks and just about anything else you care to mention. Call them gangs if you like, but friendly gangs – if that is possible. We proved that you could be competitive yet friendly at the same time.

More people, more fun and laughter. More adventure, more competition and challenges. More trouble and more disasters. And of course finding out more about ourselves. Accent, IQ, background, father's job didn't come into it. I suppose we had leaders but I can't recall that they were too dominant. If kids didn't agree, they'd peel off and form temporary mini-gangs.

That's it then. We had 'gangs of convenience,' enriching our lives every time we met up. And just occasionally girls managed to creep into some of them.

*

"It's getting too small, Jack."

"We'll need to make our den a bit bigger."

"The flames from the fire are licking me legs as I crawl past."

Further development work was now needed on our den.

"How about trying a tree-house again?" piped up 'Digger' Johnson. He was quickly shouted down.

"Belt up, Digger, remember how we nearly all died when the last one came crashing down in the hazel trees."

"Oh yer," belatedly thought one of the not-so-with it lads.

"And anyway, other gangs can see them miles away," uttered someone else.

So we decided to stay with our well tried and tested formula of a den underground. The boys of Guilden Sutton were famous for them. Pits were dug, roughly six feet square, covered with rusty corrugated sheeting that had been left lying around by house builders and then expertly camouflaged with branches and soil.

It was in our dens that we gave vent to our inventiveness and inner thoughts. Our fertile minds went into overdrive. Nothing felt impossible as we hatched plots and dreamt dreams. Landing on the moon one week, swimming the Atlantic Ocean the next. The fact that rationing was in place did little to curb our imaginations. In fact it was probably having the opposite effect. Shortages were commonplace, but so what.

"What you've never 'ad, you won't miss," echoed through most households.

I'd have been rich if I'd got a penny every time that was mentioned in our house.

Now we were having to contemplate increasing the size of our latest den in the wood just across the road from my house. It was one of my favourite woods – mature oaks and elms, small ponds and thick impenetrable bushes, criss-crossed with a maze of narrow paths, most of which were known only to gang members.

And yet it was near enough to hear Mother's shrill voice.

"Kenneth, Tony, Sheila, Jean, I won't tell you again. For the last time. It's on the table and going cold!'

Strange how I could pick up her instructions amidst the hubbub going on in and around our camp.

As the last spoonful of rice pudding followed steak and kidney pie down my 'red lane,' as often described by Father, I picked up an apple, slammed the back door and rushed back to the woods. Occasionally we supplemented home cooking with stuff cooked up in old pans over an open fire. Naturally, it always tasted terrific.

"We're going to need a much bigger sheet of corrugated iron for the roof."

So said everyone in turn as our tiny little brains clicked into action. As if by magic, instinctively we all knew what to do next.

"I'm off to get me spade," shouted 'Digger' as he darted from the wood, whilst 'Kellogg' started clearing away the soil to pull out the old sheeting.

And the rest of us scattered, either to raid sheds for saws, shears, man-size axes and the like or to begin gathering up suitable camouflage material.

Whilst this was going on small working parties set out to booby-trap the paths around. Scarily deep holes were covered with a latticework of branches and covered over with soil. Rarely did our rival gangs fall for them but it did cross my mind that adults walking their dogs might be slightly inconvenienced, to put it mildly.

"Blimey, if that Mrs Griffith from Heath Bank comes a cropper. Don't bear thinkin' about!"

My irregular pocket money would become even more irregular.

We hated Mrs G and she was the most feared member of the local KGB network of nosy neighbours. The discreet movement of her net

31

curtains normally signalled that she was back on duty.

To my little sister she was 'the Witch'. She fed info back to our parents at breakneck speed, faster than pizza deliveries today.

And the bad news continues. She also lived right next to one of our favoured play areas, the local railway bridge. Gang rivalry at this location became more muted. It was a place where boy met girl, acts of bravado were performed and young peacocks made their first diffident thrusts.

*

"We ain't played the disappearing parcel trick lately, have we, Dave?"

"Great idea."

"I'll quickly cobble together a fancy-looking box. The biggest I can find."

"That will attract 'em nicely," I thought.

"And I'll get a long piece of string from me dad's shed right away," said Jack, speeding away on his brand new bike. "Me dad won't miss it. He's got tons for holding up his fancy dahlias."

Jack was the only lad that seemed to have new things bought him. His mum, a rare Londoner in the north at that time, always found enough money to kit out her three children in brand spanking new clothes, despite her husband being an ice-cream salesman. We wondered how she managed it. Of a night time I would see her heading for Chester by herself on the bus. "Mutton dressed as lamb and so lah-de-dah," uttered many a jealous neighbour. Most of us had to make do with hand-me-downs from big sisters and brothers. Unless it was a special treat for birthday or Christmas.

Hopping onto our bikes we were quickly down by the bridge where the lane crossed over the top of the railway close to Mrs Griffith's house at the end of Heath Bank.

Our pulses began to rise out of control for fear of being caught. But it was worth the risk once in a while. And sharing the excitement with close mates heightened the sensation.

Dave carefully placed the brown paper covered box just in the gutter where it could be seen by all, tucking the string out of sight in the grass. Meanwhile I led the rest of the string under the rickety wooden fencing by the side of the bridge and down the batters towards the lines. Jack, having hidden the bikes in the long grass in the field nearby, raced across the bridge and hid in a crouched position so I could see him and he could let me know when someone was approaching. Walkers, bikers, mums pushing prams and the rare car that occasionally passed by were all fair game for our dastardly trick.

We were set. Other kids, that had come to join in the fun, secreted themselves away from view in the surrounding fields. Just as the victims stooped down to claim their new-found wealth, Jack gave me the signal. I took off. Low and behold, one high speed parcel would disappear round the end of the bridge and down the grassy bank, out of sight.

Reactions were mixed. Some victims would continue as if nothing had happened, embarrassed and not wishing to be seen profiteering from someone's loss. But often we had to handle a bit of flak.

"Cheeky little buggers."

"I'll skin you alive if I catch you."

"You'll feel the weight of my walking stick if I get you."

These would have all been better forms of punishment than if we had been recognised by Mrs G, and our parents told. That would have spelt real trouble. I recall the occasional chase by strangers to the lane, running for all their worth along the railway lines. Fortunately they always gave up defeated when it became obvious that local knowledge meant that we could blend into nature like a fox going to ground. It was all relatively harmless fun.

*

But not so the crossing of the railway bridge. In unconventional ways. Most of us had either crawled or walked in a stooped position across along the sandstone-topped walls running along either side. It was bit more challenging on a bike. Crowds arrived when the stakes increased.

"Blimey, they're doin' it on their bikes!"

Word spread like wildfire.

Several of us did it when our adrenaline was running for whatever crazy reason and it was always a great relief to get to the other side of the track, seeing the welcoming grass of the batters rising quickly towards us at the end of the wall. A fall then would have been but a minor incident. Bent handlebars, maybe a scrawpt knee.

The real heroes, the idiots and my little sister Jean, were the very few that groped their way along on the outside of the wall on a parapet no more than six inches wide, completely exposed to the sight of the twin rail tracks some twenty feet below. I recall one serious fall, resulting in a broken leg. But it would have been a bit more than that should a train have been passing at that moment.

Falling was bad enough. The loss of face in being caught by Mrs G was far worse.

I often wondered if she had a real job or was put on this earth just to protect us from ourselves. I suppose every community can accept one nosy neighbour. But only one. Mrs Griffith was ours and very successful she was, I'm sure, in saving many young lives. We always felt that she must have bypassed her own youth, and visited Moscow too often.

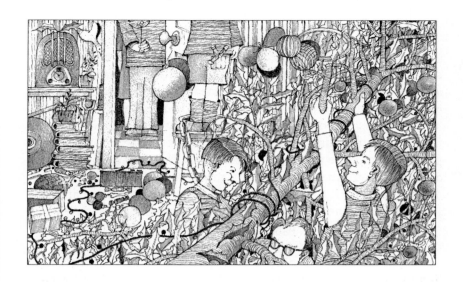

Chapter 5

Christmas time

We waited patiently for the signal from my parents.

"Our friends have got theirs up already."

We badgered away at them until they relented.

"All right, all right. The weekend."

Up the ladder into the darkness of the loft we scampered, taking unsteady steps along the rafters, avoiding the perilously flimsy plastered laths and stumbling between Father's extensive book collection. The outside of the boxes was never a pretty sight, with a goodly layer of cobwebs, dust, dead wasps and flies that had gathered in the intervening year. But who cared about the forlorn-looking cardboard boxes. We didn't. It was the contents we wanted to get our hands on.

The Christmas decorations. They never lost their sparkle year after year. Bright, dazzling, underpant-wetting excitement. We all loved

Christmas. The annual hanging ritual kicked in automatically. The never-ending dark brown picture railing that ran throughout the house, holding drab pictures and smart mirrors, made by Father, for the rest of the year, was now grandly festooned with alternate drapes of red and green bunting, pinned at two-foot intervals with drawing pins. No room was left untouched. Even the bathroom received a visit. And the lean-to if we had any left over.

With lots of willing hands, in the front room Father masterminded the erection of the prickly holly tree in a bucket of gravel. Just occasionally, when things were getting the better of him, our ears were best covered up.

We were now ready for our annual moment of real suspense.

Will they, won't they light up at the first attempt?

Laughter and tears in equal amounts were assured.

You would have thought with an electrical engineer at the helm, fairy lights would have been a doddle. Any remark from his increasingly impatient children was met with a stony look.

"Of course I know what I'm doin'. I teach the damn subject. Now let the dog see the rabbit. Everything will be champion."

It was some time later that I began to appreciate his flawed logic. Armed with his Avometer, soldering iron and coils of wire, a complete rewind of the transformer on the eve of the big day was easily within Father's compass. But we were not impressed until the lights were up on the tree. And working properly, shining brightly with lots of tinsel and baubles to keep them company.

And crackers, the contents of which Jean knew off by heart. We recycled our favourite snowmen, Santas and reindeer when they gave up the ghost, by carefully cutting out the offending filament and gluing in small torch bulbs with Durofix, the super-glue of the 1950s.

*

"Want you all up at crack of dawn and ready to go by eight. Off you go. Bricks bin in a long time so all your beds should be warm."

Having finished our prayers by the fireside, Father rattled out last-minute instructions as we sloped off to bed.

Next day was the annual Christmas pilgrimage. To Liverpool. To shop. It was largely to seek out 'girlie' things for Jean and Sheila, skirts, blouses, coats, shoes and the like, with precious little on offer for a young lad. I had no option. A three-line whip from Father meant no excuses would be considered.

At least the day started on a high with a steam-train ride from Chester General Railway Station to Birkenhead Woodside.

"And keep 'ed in lad when a bridge comes up. Don't want any visits to hospital today, do we?"

"He wouldn't miss his," Jean added, giggling away.

We normally went on the Underground beneath the River Mersey, but occasionally took the ferry. It was then that my mood changed for the worse. Out of the gloom appeared Liverpool Pier Head and the large Liver building. Bleak, grey nothingness. And a howling gale with rain could be guaranteed. Mingling with thousands of busy people on slippery cobblestones did little to settle me down.

"When we goin' home, Mum?"

"Come on son, buck up. We'll get to model shop as soon as girls are done," Father said, not entirely with conviction. Secretly, he was just as keen to see the back of rows and rows of clothes and would have been happier delving round in an ironmongery or a chandler's shop. Or staying home, pottering in his lean-to.

My spirits lifted temporarily as we entered the brightly lit, warm departmental stores. Lewis's, T.J. Hughes and C&A Modes became household names that we routinely trudged round. And, reassuringly, the unruly-looking maze of wires that whizzed wooden cups to and from the cash points to what looked like an eagle's eyrie, perched high above the milling crowd, was still there.

"That's called the rapid wire system," big brother informed me, never missing the opportunity to keep me in my place.

I often wanted to ask the assistants if I could pull their spring loaded catapult. But never plucked up enough courage.

"Mum, Mum! The Grotto – it's over there and Santa's outside with a big sack."

"Just a minute, Kenneth. We've come in here for clothes for your sisters."

"Yes, buzz off," they added in unison, poking rude faces at me through the clothes dangling on the racks.

My brother smirked as I was getting it in the neck again, and busied himself on tiptoe, looking for anything that might be interesting in other parts of the store.

Eventually, after much 'umming and arring', we drifted towards counters displaying all sorts of exciting toys that I would love to have found in my stocking on Christmas Day. Once I'd made it clear what my favourite was, we would shuffle off, but not before Mother and Father had had a bit of a chat, culminating in a wooden cup being discharged across the shop.

"What d'you think they've bought us?" I asked Tony, the oracle.

"No idea, but I bet Jean will know by tonight."

She got to know all the hiding places Mother and Father used for presents. Inside rolls of lino in the attic was most popular. Now it was full bore to the Grotto where at last all four of us were on the same wavelength. We emerged gleefully clutching an assortment of colouring books, chalks and crayons, balloons and the like, in our grubby little hands. A bit of bartering went on with my sisters but Tony would remain aloof and felt that Santa had recognised his seniority in giving him exactly what he wanted. And of course the best.

With stomachs rumbling and the party beginning to flag a little, Mother would search out a small café. This was a blessed relief for all but Father made sure we didn't get used to the idea of resting with a gentle reminder that we hadn't come all this way just to sit on our backsides. Then it was a bit more of the same and come mid-afternoon, he would pointedly look at his watch, and began making encouraging sounds.

"Better beat workers going home. Pier Head next stop, eh?"

It was not a question but a strong suggestion. There were few dissenters, what with our little aching legs and Mother's swollen feet. And not to mention the burgeoning shopping bags that I always managed to avoid carrying. If there was time, one last treat was an ice-cream from a Walls' trike at the side of the road. Of course, we never rejected them, but I often felt a bit strange licking away on something so cold whilst frostbite was setting in on various bits of my body.

The train journey home was a quiet, reflective time; I was tired and dreaming what Santa might bring me. And Sheila did her party piece, time and time again.

"Honestly, I really, really did see a shop window dummy. Still in its bright red dress and just poking out of a pile of bricks on the bomb-damaged site near to Lewis's."

We all wanted to believe her, because she was proud of her discovery, but we did wonder. Tony, less dramatically, pressed his face against the streaming wet window, scanning the Wirral skyline for wildlife. Jean would be well into eyeing up the parcels and how best to open them without being found out. Mother, having kicked off her shoes with great ceremony and relief, drifted in and out of a coma as she rested her weary body whilst Father ambled up and down the carriage, looking for newspapers left by fellow rail travellers.

Perhaps trips to Liverpool weren't quite as bad as the nightmares they gave me beforehand.

*

It was the only night of the year that Mother didn't have to chase us all up to bed.

Christmas Eve.

Bodies quickly scrubbed, teeth brightly brushed, pyjamas tugged on without prompting, we excitedly took up our ritualistic kneeling position by the fireside and did what all good Catholics were supposed to do.

"Hurry up, Dad, and not too long tonight, please."

I can't remember profound utterances coming from either Mother or Father. Normal 'Our Fathers' and 'Hail Marys' were trotted out on automatic. Just occasionally, a death, an illness or accident warranted an extra prayer or two. And of course we said an extra prayer for snow to fall.

"The family that prays together, stays together."

That's what it was all about. What the Church said, good followers like my parents tried to stick to. We might have laughed, maybe had our giggling fits, pulled funny faces at one another, but I have no doubt that those few, relatively peaceful moments of reflection, that recreation of a warm womb and the comforting muted crackling of the open fire, worked away on my subconscious as I climbed wearily up the wooden hills to bed.

Pity I couldn't have thanked my parents there and then for the loving atmosphere that they generated by their unselfish acts. But handling such thoughts is not on the agenda of one so young. In later life my parents saw the fruits of their labour come through as their family extended and further extended. They wore their obvious pride quietly on their faces.

*

"Hang on though. Santa's on his way."

How we marvelled that one solitary person could find time to visit every chimney pot in the land, laden down with so many presents.

We believed it for ages, driven by fears of fallow times.

"And he only gives them to good children."

"And what happens if there is a fire?"

"Will our chimney be big enough?"

"I hope he understood my writing."

"His reindeer might get run over!"

Our misplaced expectations every year led us to hang up at the end of the bed, the largest white pillow slips we could find in the airing cupboard. They were big enough for a plethora of seasonal goodies.

If only. Maybe this year because it didn't come last. The excited banter between our bedrooms slowly ebbed away as sleep took hold.

"He's been, he's been!"

Jean, in her over-size white nightie, popped her little bedraggled head around my door, dragging newfound wealth behind her along the landing. Big sister Sheila and Tony were also on the move.

"Quiet, it's only four," sagely added my big siblings.

Huddling together in our dressing gowns as far away from my parents' room as possible, wrapping paper was torn asunder in the gloom, lifted only by the glow of the street gaslights struggling through the curtains.

The adrenaline rush was temporally put on hold as the house resounded to Father's not-so-dulcet voice.

"I won't tell you lot again. 'Tis five and twenty to nine."

We panicked, did what we had to do, grabbed our bikes, pumped up flat tyres and the Wilbraham family were rapidly heading for Mass at St Werburgh's in Chester. We listened to another long boring sermon, took a quick look at Jesus in the crib, and enjoyed a comparison of surprises and disappointments with mates on the steps of the church. Then it was back on our bikes and pedalling 'hell for leather' all the way home.

*

The house was gradually filling with the smell of one of our favourite chickens that had had its neck pulled for the Christmas dinner table.

Turkey was still only a distant country to us.

Henrietta this time. Which one next? Perky probably.

We didn't linger long in the kitchen where Mother, slowly being hidden by a mountain of carrots, spuds and sprouts, might have waylaid us.

"They don't peel themselves, you know," she said with resignation but not really expecting us to lift a finger to help.

"Don't forget the kisses on the sprouts," we cheekily added, as we sprinted by.

A great pot of gravy blubbed away incessantly at the back of the stove.

Picking up the odd mince pie here and there, it was back to the presents.

"Do her arms really move?"

"Yer. And her legs too."

"And her head."

"Look," Jean said proudly, demonstrating the extraordinary double-jointed nature of her new pride and joy.

She was showing off her baby doll from Uncle Bill. He'd brought two or three back when he returned from Germany where he'd been an army dispatch rider during the war.

"Her eyes. Look at them close when I put my Lilly Marlene down to sleep."

I was really impressed.

Tony and myself began setting up our train set in the front room, extended by 'jumble sale' track Santa had managed to find, to run round the back of the sofa, under the table and along the front of the fireplace. Old people that turned up had to be warned regularly to tiptoe around the place for fear of making the Flying Scotsman late or causing a major derailment.

My father's dad oozed warmth and friendliness. Quickly settling into the most comfortable armchair in the house that fitted him like a well-worn overcoat, he stoked up his pipe with freshly cut twist 'baccy' and puffed away to his heart's content. His knees were ever receptive to a young child who wanted to hear him talk about his days as a young man.

"Did you really have to walk eight miles every day to that mill, Granddad?"

"And walk back again in the evening?"

"You must have been so strong and brave."

"I saw you working on your allotment yesterday."

"Did you grow the flowers you brought Mum today, Granddad?"

"And why do you push that wooden handcart everywhere you go?"

His answers were short but clear. He continued contentedly sucking on his pipe as his eyes were drawn mesmerically to the blazing open fire. He loved his Christmases surrounded by youngsters.

Father, as usual, was pretending to be in overall control of proceedings, cracking open windows to prevent the kitchen becoming like a sauna and fiddling around with the wireless aerial to ensure good reception for the Royal speech at three o'clock. Our world had to stop for that event and even a cough at the wrong time was met by raised eyebrows from the rest of the family. Knowing what we know today about the Royal House of Windsor, my father certainly wouldn't have been so deferential. But Mother would have remained loyal as neighbours said how much she looked like the Queen Mum. Father created a great song and dance of bringing coal and logs in from his stockpiles outside, blaming other people if he left a trail of debris and always made out that he'd endured arctic conditions as he blew life back into his hands, standing right in front of the fire.

"Blowing a right a gale out there. Might have a white Christmas after all, kids."

"Airing your knowledge again, eh, Charlie?"

Oh, yes, he was doing all the important jobs whilst Mother was juggling in her tiny kitchen with the small matter of providing a special meal for any number between six and sixteen, the final number depending upon the state of the weather and better offers.

*

It was later in the afternoon as lethargy was setting in. Chestnuts were occasionally popping as they roasted slowly on the hob. Tony was tunelessly working out the intricacies of the sliding button on his shiny new Hohner harmonica.

Pomegranates had done the rounds. We all found this the most frustrating fruit ever dreamt up. Armed with pins you sort of attacked the thing but rarely made much headway. They were consigned to the bin largely still intact. The following year, these unusual fruit again made their entrance, because they were the fancy fruit of the day to have at Christmas time.

Aunt Sal's high-pitched scream from the living room woke us from our slumbers.

"Oh my God! Charlie, Charlie! The decorations! God, they're on fire."

Father appeared at the top of the stairs, holding his half hitched-up trousers with one hand and a book in the other.

"Hang on, Sal. God, a man can't get any peace nowadays," he muttered as he flushed the toilet.

But Aunt Sal was in control. Sort of. Picking up the bowl from the kitchen sink, still full of washing-up water, she flung it at the problem area. Bowl and all. That did the job, but as Father kept reminding us for years, "She damned well ruined the wallpaper with all that dirty water. All it needed was a damp cloth."

That night, we went to bed early for our special version of a 'light and sound' show. Armed with one of my favourite toys, a torch with green, red and blue slides, we all climbed into bed together, apart from Tony of course. Sheila, with her rich imagination told us scary stories and my job was to add to the plot by shining different colours on the ceiling. And making suitable noises. Jean, wedged cosily in between, asking for 'more scary bits' as she disappeared further and further down the bed.

*

"Hey kids! Got tickets again for this year's panto."

Occasionally some good came out of the firm where our dad worked. We jumped for joy and scampered out from the house to tell mates.

"Can yer dad get any more?"

"What's on?"

"Never ever bin to that theatre."

"Go on, really try hard for me."

Going with mates would have been extra special.

Sadly, it wasn't on. But they received a blow-by-blow account, with interest, when we got back. For a fleeting moment every year the Royalty Theatre in City Road, Chester seduced all four of us into a world of make-believe.

"And you behave yourselves in that fancy place."

Mother got her warning in early. After all, it wasn't supposed to be filled with people like us. Most of the time, it was the preserve of the Royal and the Rich.

Flicking through old copies of the *Picture Post* in our doctor's waiting room had rubbed that indelible message into us. Did they look pompous, camped up in their elaborately carved, bulbous gold encrusted boxes! On the left, Lord and Lady Ditchwater. Right front,

Sir Richard Ponsonby-Smythe. And so the credits went on and on and on.

But wait a mo. I'm just about to share their hallowed ground. Move over aristocrats. Here come the hoi polloi. Mind you, there were still some significant differences. We had to wait outside in a long queue. In a very long, slow moving queue. In the freezing cold wind that always seemed to howl along the canal side during winter. Pitched snowball fights often helped overcome boredom. Repeated calls by Mother did little to curb our excesses.

Finally, as the heavily sprung wooden doors beckoned, we quickly came into line. Mother hastily went through her brood, brushing us down and trying to make us look less like snowmen and more like humans.

"Do try and tidy up a little. You'll catch your death of cold sitting in wet clothes all afternoon."

The transformation was magical as we left behind the windswept cold, grey streets of Chester.

"We're in, we're in," we chanted, nearly in harmony.

The atmosphere was electric

The temperature rose.

The noise level rose.

The sense of anticipation rose.

As always happened, the next few steps always took some working out as we staggered, coats half off, across the foyer which resembled a cattle market.

"I can't read what's written on tickets," Mother trotted out, trying to demist her specs with the back of her gloves.

"Give 'em 'ere, Mum."

Helpful big brother Tony was always on hand. My sisters added to the general commotion by pointing this way and that way, and being waylaid by chin-wagging with friends. Someone eventually piped up,

"Told you so. Came this way up last year."

But now was not the time for another family feud. It was upward and onward as we worked our way towards the Upper Circle.

"The Gods again, I suppose," sighed Mother as a sea of humanity swept us along the ever-spiralling, energy-sapping staircase.

Eventually reaching our destination amongst the stars, we stopped to catch our breath and spun round to take in the scene. Mother continued her orienteering exercise, trying to guide us to our seats. Our beaming faces confronted each other, looking for reassurance that it wasn't all a dream. We'd often read about palaces in fairy tales. Now we were convinced that we'd been spirited into one.

And if the stage looked like the size of a postage stamp, and we were in the cheapest seats, who cared? We certainly didn't. Gold paint, daubed copiously around the theatre, shimmered in the floodlights.

Long, heavily pleated, wine red velvet curtains cosily hung around the walls, creating a further feeling of well-being.

To heck with what was happening in the outside world. We were inside, warm and ready to be enchanted by Jack or Red Riding Hood or Snow White or Cinderella.

We didn't mind what story was about to be told, although I did have soft spot for the unbelievably fast-growing beanstalk.

"Can't you keep still, Kenneth?"

"Have you ants in your pants?"

The bare bits of my legs were having to come to terms with the hard, prickly red velvet on the seats. Cocooned in long skirts, my sisters dismissed my whingeing with irritating flicks of their hair. I tried to get even by pointing out that they were only sitting either side of Mother because they were afraid of being scared by the baddies.

Mother's stern look ended that spat abruptly. And in the event, the lowering of the lights at that point acted like magic in bringing relative silence to the place for the first time since we'd arrived.

The musicians, sitting very snugly in the appropriately named pit, started up. As the pantomime got underway, distractions disappeared and it was full focus on the stage as characters came and went.

The swirling blue haze of smoke, lit by the floodlights, intensified.

We lived uncomplainingly in a world full of chain smokers, oblivious of any shortcoming that might be just around the corner. Any mention of the effects of 'secondary smoking' would have confined you to the loony bin indefinitely.

We joined in the ritual 'behind you,' hissing at the baddies, and were charmed out of our seats by the hero and heroine. At half time, sweets and ice-cream, by kind permission of Father's firm, circulated along the rows.

My sisters were always terrified that they would be yanked out of the audience to perform something. Fat chance of that ever happening with the stage a good bus ride away. However, it never entirely allayed their fears and occasionally preys on their minds to this day.

We were all at exhaustion-point as the stage filled for final bows and the curtains closed with a great flourish. It took us several days to readjust to the less glitzy world of village life.

And I bet my mates were glad when I finally stopped rabbiting on about what they'd missed yet again.

Chapter 6

Fireworks

"Charlie! Charlie, go and see what that oldest lad of yours is up to in garage. He's making a heck of a smell and the noise is getting me down. Up to no good, I reckon, I'm sure."

"Dinna fass yerself, Nell. Fireworks, that's what he's up to. Gunpowder, treason and plot and all that. Becoming a bit of a wizard making 'em."

"You wouldn't say that if he blew his hands off. Or made a hole in that garage roof you've yet to finish."

"He's all right. Lad knows what he's doin'. A bit like me. Can't do much harm and he's got to get them ready for tomorrow."

The bonfire had been steadily growing for the past month in the back garden. The same was happening in every other garden down the lane. Later, and after our plum tree had been partly incinerated on more than one occasion, we would have communal fires on waste land nearby. But for now we had great fun building our own, from anything we could get our hands on, which often continued burning brightly deep into the night.

My hard-earned pocket money went into buying a few sparklers and green and red Bengal matches. Father forked out for Catherine Wheels that always needed a helping hand to spin round, Jumping Jacks, rockets and the like.

We scurried into the garage.

"Cor, you've made lots."

"What'll that one do?"

"Will it bang?"

"What colours are there?"

Tony continued working away diligently in the gloom, on the heavily battle-scarred wooden bench. Neat piles of sulphur, charcoal, iron filings, potassium chlorate and ammonium dichromate lay before our resident alchemist.

His line of bangers resembled little twisted salt bags found in crisp packets. But there the similarity ended.

"Stand back. Right back, you lot."

Placing them on a hard surface, he achieved ignition by swinging the yard brush through a wide arc. An ear shattering explosion occurred.

More bristles fell to the ground. Once the brush head began to split, it was time to look around for another. Father gave a resigned look, impressed with his son's inventiveness which had been achieved at some cost to his possessions.

"Be sure to wrap up well. All of you."

"I don't want you catching a death of cold."

Mother gave us the mandatory once-over. Balaclavas, snug woolly scarves wrapped round and round and round, duffel coats, gloves on strings, two pairs of socks and wellies.

"Ready for the North Pole," Father predictably chipped in as he worked his feet into his old leather boots. They had seen better days but he still meticulously dubbined them every now and again.

Torches, waved wildly, mystically lit up our super-charged breath hitting the cold night air. Mother's treacle toffee started doing the rounds.

"Hey. The guy! He's alight."

It was always a special moment. After all, in his major role as 'penny for the guy,' he'd been our passport to a few riches as we hawked him around the neighbours for the last few days. Now he was nearly no more.

As the fire settled down and a deep red bed of embers began forming, it was time for the spuds. We would roll them into position with long sticks and then wait.

And wait. And wait.

And what were we waiting for?

When we recovered them, they resembled small rocks, with ash-stained, carbonised skin. Ah, but split open and a fork full of butter, they had gourmets of the day salivating. Next morning we would continue our search for more spuds.

Chapter 7

Behind and in front of every good man

At Number 40 another conflict of interests was beginning to loom. A normally chaotic household was once again in danger of becoming totally out of control.

"Charlie, how many more times will I tell you? That room. There's stuff everywhere. And guests expected. Get it finished. Otherwise, I'll get someone in."

"Nonsense, Nell. You know no one else can do it properly. And they'd charge the earth in t'bargain."

"Well then, if it isn't done by weekend I'll get some paint from town and do it with the kids."

"You'll do nothin' of the sort. Leave me be and I'll get round to it."

Our cuddly mum, not much over five feet tall but making up for it in girth size, was having one of her infrequent, but effective well-timed outbursts to keep Father in check.

And we kids could also get the same sort of brusque treatment when bickering and rising tempers threatened family harmony: "You lot. Outside. Immediately. Get yourself a good dose of fresh air."

She was magically efficient when the need arose and rarely lost her temper. We were all aware, Father included, just where we stood and where our next meal was coming from. She doubled up as a nurse when illness struck and sent us all happily into the Land of Nod every night with our favourite bedtime stories.

*

Much of what my mother stood for was firmly rooted in having lived through two world wars and also being the product of parents who could hardly have been more different. Her father was an Irish soldier, always full of bonhomie and surrounded by fawning cronies in his local pub which became a second home. Her mother came from well-to-do Cheshire farming stock. My mother was never keen to visit the potentially interesting bit of family history of how they became man and wife.

Alcohol was always a sensitive topic with her and the nearest she ever got to it was when she used the occasional dash of brandy for preserving her much sought-after fruit cakes. Tea and fruit juices were the only drinks offered to visitors at our house and she tried to avoid going to those relatives and friends who could only wheel out the drinks trolley.

"That's not the right way to welcome people. A cup of tea is far more sensible," she would quietly mouth when out of earshot of our hosts.

No doubt her firmly-held views were strongly linked to experiences in the old part of Chester, strangely named Newtown, where she was born. A new town no doubt once, but to me it was always old. It was classic back-to-back terraced housing as far as the eye could see, with a pub virtually on every street corner. The city could boast one pub for every day of the year and that could only have meant one thing. Heavy drinking.

At first hand Mother saw the terrible havoc it brought to many families. She was a great supporter of the Salvation Army who toured the pubs in her neighbourhood, particularly on a Friday night, in an attempt to knock a bit of sense into men hell-bent on peeing their last penny in the gutter or against a wall. As an antidote to her drunken father, our mother must have gained some relief in seeing her mother adding something to the community when she set up a small shop in her front room of their house on the corner of Wellington Street and Henry Street.

She was typical of tens of thousands of women up and down the land. Unsung heroines who maintained a semblance of order as their menfolk fought for their country. For a large part of her life, males dominated. Most women finished work to have a family. And that was that. No going back. Tied by unforgiving apron strings to the sink, the cooker, the boiler and ironing board. And endless other chores.

Every hour of every day of every week was spoken for. No need for a diary, and if they'd been available, Mother would have found more use for the pages of a Filofax strung up in the lavatory. Maternity leave was still light years away. And as for men being given time off when another nipper arrived on the scene, Father would have been in no doubt.

"Give over lad. Have thy gone potty? With thoughts like that, thy should be in loony bin."

*

Attending the needs of four children from crib to workplace, took her out of circulation to such an extent that Mother's confidence was eroded and her social skills became rusty. Like so many mothers, she struggled in obstinate silence after we had all flown the nest.

Slowly, but surely, she started to find herself again. She threw herself into action with the local Women's Institute. Her cooking skills, honed from working at Griffiths the Bakers in Northgate Street, Chester, stood her in good stead. A regular winner in the local cooking competitions, she could never pass on precise tips. When asked what she had done, it was a question of, "Well my dear, a handful of this, a bit more of that, not too much of the other."

Cooking time was "take it out when it looks ready, my dear."

It was one way of keeping her trade secrets, not that this subterfuge, I'm sure, ever occurred to her.

"Go on, Mum. Tell us again what happened at that famous school buffet lunch."

"Well, I just happened to casually remark to a friend that the sausage rolls looked a bit dingy and unappetising."

"And then what, Mum?" we all chimed in, having heard it a thousand times before.

"Well, this smartly turned-out lady with a frightfully posh accent, brushing past, coolly remarked, 'I happen to have made them.'"

It only happened to be my headmaster's wife.

As kids we cared little about the composition of her food, as long as it was ready when we were hungry and that there was plenty of it. Mind you, big brother always tried to get the juicier bits onto his plate, leaving my sisters, me and Dad to take what was left, in that order. Seldom was food left, even though vegetables were regularly boiled to destruction in Saxa salt-laden water. We ate to survive, with healthy eating fads still decades away. How she rustled up meals, day after day, with so little to hand, baffled us all.

*

Mothers were not allowed to become ill and ours was no exception. Father, nursing a cold or hobbling around from strained muscles, was easily taken in our stride.

As long as we recognised his slight discomfort and told him he looked better, he carried on pottering around his lean-to and garden. But Mother going down with some dreaded lurgy? No, not possible. It just was not allowed. No doubt there were countless times when she was feeling under the weather or worse, but the stoicism she possessed kept her discomfort hidden from us, fearing that we would get upset – which would have only compounded her condition.

*

"Oh my God!"

She had every right to take the Lord's name in vain as she entered my bedroom.

There I lay on a heavily-blooded pillow with little white showing – the result of a visit to the dentist to remove four molars in one go. As if being violently sick from laughing gas hadn't been enough of a penalty to pay. Now she had decisions to make after picking herself up from collapsing onto the floor. Quickly she realised I was still in this world.

Father had gone to work and three other kids needed processing. No phone, no car and a goodly walk to catch a bus. Slowly she cajoled me into some form of action, helped me dress and virtually carried me half a mile. By the time the bus dropped us off in Hoole outside the surgery, the bleeding had virtually stopped. The dentist plugged the gums and we were off home again.

Mother was no doubt more relieved than me. I only hoped it wouldn't mess up my plans to play cricket that evening with my mates.

The other occasion was the need for major internal surgery to put right what having four children had severely overtaxed. Within three weeks, however, she returned from hospital, to make the house a home once again.

In these days of so many latch-key kids, it is hard to believe that she was always in to greet us back from school. Only when she was travelling up and down the country, going from hospital to hospital with a cousin's mother, Aunt May, to find a cure for her cancer, was she out of circulation.

Perhaps the greatest achievement later in life was her painting. She enrolled at art school and found a latent talent, particularly using oils. She got great pleasure out of painting anything to do with nature, and at last she had the opportunity to discuss and work with like-minded people pursuing a hobby with passion that had been denied her for so long. We also bathed in the reflected glory as we saw Mother in a completely different light. Of course, as usual, Father had to get into the act, by framing and hanging her creations.

Chapter 8

Father found other ways in

"Talacre here we come," echoed around our house.

It signalled the end of school for the summer and the start of our yearly pilgrimage to the 'bungalhouse' situated on the sea front near to the Point of Ayr colliery in North Wales.

Nowadays it looks like a large caravan park, but in the Forties and Fifties it was a rare haven for those fortunate enough to be able to go on holiday in a country still reeling from war and its aftermath. We were one of those rare fortunate families.

Not that we had much more money than the average family in the village. But we had a very enterprising father and an even more understanding and accommodating mother.

Preparations were all important for this annual event. No sooner had we arrived home from Talacre than my parents were thinking about the following year.

Stockpiling of tinned food was the all-important factor in allowing us to move away from our house for more than the occasional day. From September onwards, Mother would start the hoarding operation. Beans, peas, spaghetti, corned beef, ham and soup were core items.

With rationing still very much in force, it was a considerable achievement on the part of Mother to gather together enough food to sustain six hearty appetites for up to four weeks in the bracing sea air of Talacre. As the year wore on, piles of food would form under the stairs, in the bedrooms and anywhere else that there was space in a very overcrowded house, already bulging with books and all things mechanical.

With a large family, transport was also another key consideration. From Chester General railway station, trains ran right along the North Wales coast to Holyhead in Anglesey. They operated relatively frequently, but the journey times were unbelievably long for the relatively short distance to Talacre. No sooner had the engine got up a head of steam than it was applying its brakes for the next station.

"Blimey, we're not stopping again are we?"

"We'll never get there," we all sighed down the carriage.

It felt that there were dozens of stations between Chester and Talacre and yet they were separated by less than 40 miles, running up the west side of the Dee estuary.

Any self-respecting youngster in those days spent the larger part of a rail journey with his or her head out of the carriage window. I never lost any friends through decapitation by tunnels or signalling gear, so it was a relatively safe pastime and it made the journey go so much faster.

Inevitably, my sisters, brother and myself would arrive with blackened faces and my mother would have to apply copious amounts of 'golden eye' ointment to remedy the effects of smoke, grit and soot picked up during the journey.

As we grew older and our interests widened, the train proved inadequate for our needs. By the time we had assembled six bikes, dozens of boxes of food, kites, model aircraft, sand digging equipment and sports gear to cover a wide range of climatic conditions, it was a logistical nightmare.

This was where my father's enterprise and my mother's understanding came to the fore.

"I'll get lorry organised again, eh, Nell?"

We never did get to know the full story of where the vehicle came from, but it duly turned up on time year after year, complete with a driver for the journey.

It could well have been carrying coal or soft drinks for the remainder of the year. The first task was to convert it into what we nowadays call a 'people carrier' not very far removed from those you see today parked in their thousands outside fancy schools and also now the not-so-fancy schools, up and down the country.

It was a flat-backed vehicle, having hinged sides and imitating a very large shallow box.

The main modification was the erection of a tarpaulin over the top, mainly to keep the elements out but, I suspect, also to hide the blushes of my mother.

"Hurry up, Charlie, before the neighbours see us," she would say, trying as discreetly as possible to chivvy Father along.

Our departure from the village was certainly not a low-key affair.

"When you goin' on hols?" we were asked by our mates time and time again.

I suspect it was not to wish us well but to get a definite date for the return of the sports equipment that we were temporarily removing from circulation. By the time it came to moving away from the house, a fair number of people had assembled to wave us off.

The journey time was around two hours.

How those last miles took so long as we approached the coast.

Turning off the main North Wales coast road, we found ourselves on a heavily potholed lane. A gently sloping bridge, presumably built with horse and carts in mind, then took us sedately over the railway track by Talacre station.

"I saw the sea first!" was the normal chant from one of my sisters as we hit the unmade road leading up to the 'bungalhouse'.

The term bungalhouse was the agreed name for our dwelling following countless arguments as to whether it was a house or a bungalow.

All eyes were now on finding the defunct green double-decker bus on the left-hand verge.

No ordinary bus, but one that had seen better days and now, having been put out to grass, it acted as the local post-office, ice cream vendor and supplier of buckets and spades to visitors.

Once there, it was right-hand down and into the large garden surrounding the bungalhouse.

The lorry had hardly stopped when we jumped over the side looking for our friends that we hadn't seen since the previous year. As our parents unloaded the vehicle, we would race inside to bag our favourite bedrooms and then back out again to sort the sports gear and set up the pitch for a game of football.

Seemingly within minutes, friends would be shouting to us from the nearby sand-dunes whilst others would fight their way through great wild swathes of arching sprays of orange-flowered montbretia that surrounded the lawn.

And when we heard the distinctive yell, "Calor Gas van man calling," this was confirmation indeed that we really were on holiday.

*

"Wot, bin to a colliery? Thought you were on holiday," Dave muttered.

"I was, but my dad always talks his way into interesting places wherever we go. Well, he thinks they are interesting."

"Yer, well, was it interesting?"

"Yep, it was great," I replied.

It was a ritual, every year. An integral part of our long summer holidays in Talacre on the North Wales coast.

Getting to the colliery was, in itself, an adventure.

Once on the beach after a short walk from our bungalhouse, with the proud, faded whitewashed eighteenth century lighthouse to our left, we struck out south-east past some of our favourite playing areas. Long, undulating sand dunes that grew and shrank at the whim of the wind, ceaselessly being pounded away.

Some resistance was offered by the stout prickly saltwort, sand couch and marram grass. These muscular, pioneering colonists tied invisible knots in the sand. Anchored well down, they kept our playground intact.

As the dunes petered out we continued along a narrow, meandering causeway.

We became very familiar with this path, for it was our only lifeline back to civilisation once the tide had surged in.

Occasionally we came across visitors wading back, water up to their chests and worse. Arms in the air carrying what they wanted to keep dry. Hopefully.

A bit of local knowledge and even at the highest tide we only got our knees wet. But until we got back to the dunes, we couldn't relax for fear that the sea had devoured part of our secret, sunken path. I dread to think what thoughts went through my mother's mind.

As we approached the colliery, we could see single-hatched coasters hovering on the horizon, waiting patiently to take away another load of cannel coal.

It was still a time in the country when we couldn't mine enough to fuel the ever-increasing demand for power.

Steam was very much king.

Wherever we went, my father always did his homework beforehand. It was same Dad that got us into pumping stations, the engine rooms of boats, the inner sanctums of abbeys and churches, into dungeons and lofts, and through doors often labelled 'private' or 'no entry.'

*

Now it was the turn of a colliery to receive us.

I was never particularly interested in what my father was saying to the first line of resistance that met us on such occasions. At times he was positively embarrassing for us.

"What's he up to now? Who's he talking to?" my mother enquired of us children, knowing that we had no idea either.

"Probably telling the man that he knows a man who is related to the manager of wherever we were trying to get into," I often reflected with my siblings later.

Everything appeared so huge as we traipsed single file into Point of Ayr colliery that first time, following our leader through the barrack-like gates. Wherever I looked, coal piles were being manipulated into shape by huge machines, roving round like an army of ants.

My father had a nose for going to the right place straight away. Leaving us, already ankle deep in mud and coal dust, he headed meaningfully towards a half-open door in a small building, nestling in the shadow of the imposing winding room with two enormous rotating wheels held aloft. I didn't expect him to get much change from a derelict-looking building with whitewashed windows that must have let in as much light as the surrounding weathered brickwork.

Minutes that seemed like hours went by and then he emerged alongside a helmeted man.

"OK kids, Mr Jones has said that we can go and see his canaries."

He looked smug, having pulled it off.

Again.

Mother was relieved that our trek had been productive, knowing that failure would have resulted in four very long faces all the way back to the bungalhouse.

Make that six very long faces.

Expectations rose as our new friend handed round white hats just like he had, and then gave us a friendly chat on what we could do and what we couldn't do now we were on National Coal Board property. Vesting Day in 1947 had seen coal become the property of the people.

The air was alive to an amazing mix of noises.

Most of the activity centred around the winding room sitting over the pit shaft that went down several thousand feet, and then five miles horizontally out under the sea.

Here, I looked in awe at the queuing miners preparing for battle, donned in orange overalls, heavy black leather belts holding batteries, steel toe-capped boots, well-used looking helmets carrying lights, gnarled leather knee pads and gloves.

And of course their 'snap tins' which more often than not contained thick slices of bread coated in jam or dripping, prepared no doubt by their kitchen-bound wives.

With a somewhat resigned look, they offered themselves for a final check over by the pit 'deputy' for cigarettes and matches, and were given an identity tag.

Once the hoist operator heard the 'all clear' bell signal from the bottom of the shaft, they were sent on their way to the centre of the earth in a flimsy, Meccano-style open structure cage, alongside empty coal tubs and steel pit-props which were rapidly replacing well worn wooden ones.

It was certainly not a job for the fainthearted.

Amidst a great amount of clanging of bells, the same men would reappear some eight hours later, blackened corpses with eyes like faintly flickering searchlights, breaking through the gloom. Brimming tubs of hard-won coal in adjacent cages were testimony to their toil. Little wonder that few miners encouraged their sons to follow them underground.

*

"Could tiddly little fragile canaries have a role to play in such a hostile environment?" I muttered to myself as we gathered pace behind Mr Jones.

Past the miners' shower facilities, strangely known as pit-head baths.

Past the organised chaos of the huge blacksmith's shop, spewing out bright orange and red flames and sparks in synch with the dull thumping of hammers in the background.

"A sort of ancient 'light and sound' show seemingly put on for our benefit," I reflected.

Past enormous heaps of weary-looking conveyor belts that had once done sterling work in moving millions of tons of coal.

Then, abruptly, rounding yet another dusty corner of yet another large desperate-looking building, we arrived at a relatively civilised, quiet part of the colliery.

'First Aid, Safety and Emergency Department,' read the notice in large red lettering.

"And you all know what we'll find in here, don't you?" asked our Mr Jones, settling comfortably into his new role as 'Manager of Site Visits by Inventive Families on Rare Holidays.'

"Canaries!" we all bellowed together.

We weren't wrong.

As the door swung open, we could see rows of breathing equipment and gas cylinders, neatly laid out against the far wall. And there to my right, cage after cage of bright yellow chirping birds.

Big brother Tony, the self-appointed ornithologist of the family, soon had a handful of seeds from heaven knows where and was offering them to the canaries through the bars. He was the only one to be given a canary egg and you can imagine what the rest of us thought about that!

We all eventually had a go at feeding and then Father of course had to break his silence when some explaining was called for.

"Listen, when there's been a fire underground, you can get pockets of a gas called carbon monoxide forming which can kill you. So the miners in the rescue parties take canaries down because they are very sensitive to this gas. If they fall off their perches, the miners know that there is danger about. So they put on their breathing apparatus."

"That's cruel!" said one of my sisters.

"The canaries will die."

"No, not at all," interrupted our official guide, not wanting any tears. "We give them a quick whiff of oxygen and they are as right as rain in next to no time."

That made us all feel much better.

"And one further treat before you go. You can all have a drink in the canteen."

Hardened, tough-looking miners, looking up from their plates, gave us a quizzical look as we entered in crocodile style.

"Wot de'ell they doing 'ere?" I could feel them saying under their breath in their singy-songy Welsh accents.

"Men trapped with nowhere else to go," I thought. Doing back-breaking work till the end of their working days. And then probably dying early with some form of lung-related illness.

Huge white, chipped enamel mugs were slammed down on the metal tables in front of us. To this day I can't remember the contents, but it was probably that celebrated northern drink, dandelion and burdock, the only liquid I recall that didn't have a utilitarian taste to it.

As we headed towards the main gates, we noticed a lonely pony grazing in a pen.

"Retired pit pony, put out to pasture," said Dad knowledgeably. "Don't need them nowadays, with the coming of the diesel engine."

We didn't disagree; my sisters made their normal doting noises and soon we had the colliery to our backs, heading home, having said our thanks to Mr Jones.

*

Often if the tide was out and our stomachs were not rumbling too much, we would race out across the sandy expanse of the Dee estuary. The beautifully sculpted surface left by the receding tide now was littered with casts from defecating lugworms and the occasional highly-collectable cuttlefish backbones, razor-shells and sea urchin cases. Tony, also our resident shell expert, built up quite a collection.

"That's where we need to go," he shouted, now back in ornithological mode, pointing to large flocks of stout-billed oystercatchers, sandpipers and dunlins.

"We'll find plenty of cockles there."

Digging quickly brought us rich rewards and we soon had stacks of them in our buckets and bags.

Sea food is all well and good but I have lingering memories of long preparation times with little to see at the end of it. Still, ownership of our rich pickings quickly passed over to Mother when we got home. Into a large pot of clean salty water went the cockles before they were boiled next day.

I wasn't particularly keen on their rubbery texture and neither were my siblings. But we did adore the Parfitt's shrimps, whose impressive ever-boiling cauldron resided the other side of a small field from our 'bungalhouse'.

Now they were a labour of love to get to the dinner table. Master P did the catching and boiling and poor old Mistress P did the shelling of the beasts.

I recall, but with a great level of uncertainty, that from about ten pounds and hours of sweat and toil she was lucky to finish up with a small plateful of shrimp meat. But boy did it taste good.

I bet my father didn't pay a proper commercial rate for them. He probably offered to do some DIY on their rundown chalet in exchange. That was Charlie, our self-contained dad.

To complete this culinary merry-go-round, and a reminder that rationing was still very much with us, seaweed also made its way to our table.

Not any old seaweed though.

'Sampkin,' my parents called it – glasswort or marsh samphire, to give it its fancy botanical name. It grew in large quantities in the heavily channelled mud flats that we often traversed on the way back from the colliery. These fascinating muddy areas were not particularly flat, in fact they were deep and dangerous.

They were largely hidden with the odd green tuft here and there at high tide. But as the water receded the mud dried with a crazy paving appearance. These dykes had an incredible pulling power for us kids. We were in our element, crawling across the slimy, slippery banks, competing with curlew and other sea birds to catch small crabs and tiddlers that had been left high and dry by the tide.

"Pop, pop, pop," was the joyous sound as we punctured long strings of bladder wrack tucked away in crevasses.

After boiling the sampkin in salted water, we would then use a fork to strip off the green fleshy segments from the thin woody twig-like matrix, add a smidgeon of vinegar, a bit more salt and as Father so often said, 'get it down the hatch.'

"I do wish you'd talk properly to the children, Charlie. They'll never learn with that sort of silly language." Another abortive attempt by Mother to get us to speak proper-like.

Today, healthy living and the anti-salt movement would make sampkin totally unpalatable. In any event, since it is now protected by the rather grand status of 'endangered plant', you will never get the opportunity to find out what you have missed!

*

A trip to a religious building was mandatory on all our family holidays. Later, castles were added to the list. Father decreed without consultation.

"Have you heard? Tomorrow we're off to Talacre Abbey," my sisters sheepishly whispered to me.

That meant a long trudge back past the railway station and up a steep hill. Far too many miles for our little legs to propel us, we all thought, except Tony who hoped to see a long-tailed, greater spotted wotsit which he hadn't yet crossed off in his immaculately-kept *Observer's Book of British Birds*.

Older sister Sheila occasionally managed to get round Father and got special permission to stay in the bungalhouse and read 'only a book that will be useful when you go back to school'. Father never let up for a moment.

Talacre Abbey wasn't really all gloom. I recall the monks as quite welcoming creatures in their flowing brown habits, moving effortlessly and quietly. The smell of incense was around every corner.

And they sold some tasty home-made pickle, chutney and jam. Despite their inflated price, Father thought it was all for a good cause.

"Must cost 'em a small fortune heating a place that size."

No one was listening to him and he seemed happy enough parting with the odd copper or two to Catholic places of worship.

Mother would buy one or two sets of rosary beads as presents and a selection of holy cards to send to favoured relatives and neighbours.

Thinking of it later, the monks, although somewhat isolated, must have had a pretty good time in between their sporadic bouts of praying. I bet they didn't go short of much!

But we hadn't escaped yet. The beach would have to wait awhile. Into the chapel we were frog-marched. Stations of the Cross to be done. Out came the rosary beads and we chanted lots of 'Hail Marys' and a few 'Our Fathers.'

By this time my sisters and I felt the giggles coming. Without fail, entering holy places always brought them on if we were together. One look from any of us was enough. A gentle titter quickly turned to rib-aching agony as we tried in vain to remain po-faced whenever Mother or Father cast their beady eyes our way.

Trying to hide behind pillars and pews out of view of them, only delayed the inevitable and at least one of us was usually sent packing in disgrace to wait outside in repentant mood.

It was imperative to put on the most serious face possible to meet the family when they eventually emerged, dipping their hands ceremoniously in the holy water font. A minute of looking sorry quickly broke the ice and family business was resumed.

All that was left was to confess the following weekend, reel off a few more 'Our Fathers' and that was that until the next time.

*

"Oh heck. Looks like Tony's having another asthma attack."

Only minutes earlier he'd been happily flying his huge yellow kite which Father had bought as 'Government surplus stock'. The wind must have got up and pulled the string out of his hands. We could hear him wheezing as he desperately raced across the sands, trying to retrieve the reel. Without any tension in the line, the kite was rapidly dropping in the sky but as soon as the reel hit the water, up it rose, dragging the reel further out to sea. Heading rapidly for Hilbre Island – and beyond. He was inconsolable. We all had a bit of weep but quickly put the disappointment behind as we got stuck into the next 'challenge'.

Something that was intended to enter the water was a message that we put into a bottle which was launched off the Talacre coast one year. Sometime later a letter arrived from a man up the Wirral saying 'thank you' for our novel way of communicating.

*

"Hey up."
"Out the way."

"Let the dog see the rabbit."

Things were not looking too good on the primus stove front. We went everywhere with our primus stove. No holiday picnic was complete unless we went through the trials and tribulations of getting the damn thing going, to boil the kettle and heat beans or spaghetti or whatever.

Father was in control. Well, after all it was a potentially dangerous piece of gear. First of all meths had to be lit to get the vaporising ring hot and then the paraffin tank had to be pressurised to produce a fine spray and hopefully a lovely big roaring circle of blue flames.

But life was never that simple.

The jet more often than not got blocked.

The pricker device for unblocking was never to hand and when found, required straightening before it was of any use.

Meanwhile the wind would have changed direction and was trying its damnedest to thwart Father's efforts by blowing the meths' pilot flame out.

"Leave you for five minutes by yourselves and look what happens," Father chuntered on to himself.

"When will kettle be boiling Charlie?" Mother innocently enquired of our nearly out-of-control leader. Father looked up and said nothing.

"Round here a bit more son. That's it."

With the windbreak now doing a good job and the stove at last in a horizontal mode, Father could relax just a little.

"Dad, can I have go at pumping the paraffin?"

Once one had a go, we all had to have a go. The smell of burning hair added to the heady atmosphere around the shining brass stove.

And we often lost track of the fact that Mother was patiently waiting in the wings trying valiantly to rustle up some hot food for six ever-open mouths.

In the end the kettle always nearly reached boiling point and moderately warm food was eventually dished out.

And we left the washing-up till we got back to the 'bungalhouse' where Mother coped admirably by herself.

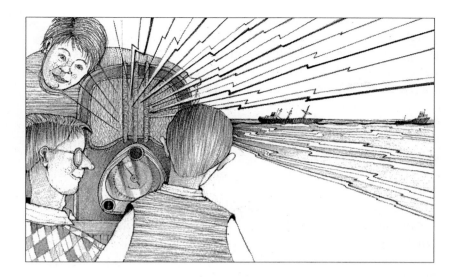

Chapter 9

Wireless drama

As soon as I saw him pass the kitchen window on his bike, I dashed out the back door to give him the news.

"Dad, dad! They've got a towrope at last onto the *Flying Enterprise*."

The battle to save the American freighter, listing badly in the Atlantic Ocean, 500 miles west of Lands End, had been making headline news in the papers and on wirelesses round the world for the past few days. Every night, with my dad and brother, I huddled round our bakelite Echo wireless on the sideboard, listening for the latest after the pips at six o'clock.

The tension had been building from that fateful Boxing Day in 1951 when a severe gale force wind lashed all before it. The *Flying Enterprise* was just one of many ships in trouble that were frantically sending out distress calls. The freighter, badly damaged, immediately rolled over at an alarming angle. The magnitude of the disaster unfolding was quickly realised by two other American ships struggling themselves to make for quieter waters. That had to wait awhile as they sped back into the teeth of the gale to help a 'friend in need'.

"Well, they ought to be thankful," Father announced to the family, when he heard all 35 members of the crew were safe and well. There were several women and children on board, presumably out for a nice cheap trip on the ocean waves. It hadn't turned out as they might have expected.

"That's not right, Dad. The captain has stayed on by himself," I butted in.

"Well, maybe there's some valuable cargo on board to look after."

"Yer, like nuclear material or blocks of gold," added my brother knowledgeably.

"Or something useful like tinned fruit that I'd like to get my hands on," added Mother with a more rational answer. As always.

I found out that the Captain was a Dane called Kurt Carlsen and the wireless reporter said he had salt, not blood in his veins. That confused me 'til big brother came to my rescue again.

A rescue tug took another week to get to the *Flying Enterprise*. In the meantime, the freighter drifting helplessly, danced to the tune being played by the hostile seas that barely let up for a moment. I gained some solace in the knowledge that an American destroyer, the *John W. Weeks* was shadowing the stricken ship. From time to time the two closed up and carefully, judging the drunken movements of the powerless ship, the destroyer successfully transferred hot food, drink and cigarettes to the beleaguered skipper. But not before several attempts had ended in failure.

I told my mum that bit when she came to tuck me up in bed.

"I'm sure he's really enjoyed that cup of tea. Warmed the cockles of his heart no doubt," Mother said reassuringly as she kissed me goodnight.

But I could hardly sleep and my thoughts kept turning to this brave man, by himself and out there in the cold, dark ocean. This was no make-believe hero that I regularly read about in comics and books. He was a real live hero, growing in stature before my very eyes as we sat down every night to hear the latest news. All the world now knew him.

Eventually the news I'd been hoping for – a brave little tug named the *Turmoil* had muscled its way from Falmouth and now had the patient in sight.

Tired, wet and working on a deck heeling over at an extreme angle, try as he could, Karlsen couldn't make secure the light lines being fired over from the tug. Time and again, fatigue got the better of him. Hurried discussions on the tug between Captain Parker and his Chief Officer, a strapping young man named Dancy, solved this immediate problem.

The wireless and newsvendor's billboards now had another hero.

"Dancy leaps to the rescue."

"The Dancy Leap."

The people of his small village near Tunbridge Wells began singing the praises of their boy, recalling him being a compulsive tree climber.

Now with help, the tug and freighter were soon as one.

Towing, at last, could begin.

Steadily, Captain Parker eased the throttles open, the *Turmoil* straightened up and began the 300-mile tow to Falmouth.

Day one passed with steady progress.

Then day two, day three. Very long days. Nervous days.

But on day four, disaster struck.

Tony had been listening to the latest news on a crystal set in his bedroom and blarted it out to all and sundry.

The savage sea had once more taunted its victim. *Turmoil*'s powerful winch swiftly retrieved the forlorn, slack tow which told its own story. Again the freighter began drifting. But the good news was that it was in the right direction. *Turmoil* and other tugs frantically worked out whether another rope could be attached. People up and down the land were willing the ship to fight and beat the wild sea.

Even the BBC eased its austere way of broadcasting and began reporting in a more animated way.

"She's still afloat. Looks like she might make it."

More billboards spread the news.

"Fifty miles to go. Still fighting."

The valves in our wireless were now in danger of over-heating.

"Please don't conk out. Not yet. Give me one more day."

My sisters couldn't understand what all the fuss was about.

"Are things bucking up, then? Or is it all doom and gloom still?" they enquired with little feeling.

That night brought more bad news I didn't want to hear. Slowly the *Flying Enterprise* was slipping. The weather was taking a turn for the worse and all hope of another towline being connected was gone.

Now it was a question of saving life. Captain Karlsen had accepted defeat.

The *Turmoil* gingerly edged up to what remained of the freighter above water and the two men precariously scrambled along to the end of the smoke-stack. They slid gently into the water, Dancy allowing Captain Karlsen the final moment alone before they clung onto one another as they bobbed up and down. Within minutes they were on board the *Turmoil*. Safe, but no doubt sad.

Karlsen went below to dry out, not wanting to see his ship finally slip away beneath the oily swell. That night I heard the sad announcement that the *Flying Enterprise*, having fought valiantly for two weeks, finally sank 40 miles off Falmouth. Nearly, but not quite.

Our wireless had given me a ringside seat to witness a glorious, never-to-be-forgotten, fight. The heroism shown by those two men was not the stuff of losers. The evil sea knew it had been in a battle and would have settled for a draw.

I never did find out what cargo the *Flying Enterprise* was carrying. No one else seemed to know. Not even my brother.

Chapter 10

Don't bet on inheritance

Out of the great melting pot of life they emerged and keep doing so. Products of a healthy, random process.

No place for designer models via genetic engineering, I say. The unknown is more exciting and challenging. I had a typical motley selection of relations thrust upon me. No complaints about that.

Variety is the spice of life, eh?

Kids being kids, I'm sure that no one in my family was ever left in any doubt as to who was a popular relative and who was not – those we burst blood vessels getting to and those that we hid from, under the table, or went missing in the garden upon their arrival.

For me the challenge was four grandparents, thirteen aunts and uncles and umpteen cousins.

Because my mother and father were the eldest in their respective families, relatives tended to gravitate to Number 40 for family gatherings, anniversaries and so on. The all-important eating arrangements, still controlled by rationing, were helped along by generous relatives, bringing the good old-fashioned staples of sugar, tea and biscuits. Corned beef from Argentina and tinned fruit from South Africa occasionally made an appearance. Foul chicory essence, an ingenious coffee-substitute, sometimes turned up. That's something Starbuck's has yet to discover.

*

"He's a rum character, he was."

You can say that again. Not many of the family would disagree.

Granddad Stanton. My mother's dad. William Staunton really but what's the dropping of a 'u' between friends?

Lying about his age, this staunch Irishman joined the army to break-in wild horses needed for war duty. He was tough as old boots, contemptuously brushing aside double pneumonia when he was well into his eighties.

"I'll be up in a day or two," he boasted between coughing fits.

He was.

"He loved his horses more than his family," Mother often recalled.

After discharge from the army, he had many jobs, including that of a night watchman at the Summers Steel works. I often visualised him, huddled over a glowing brazier near the main gates of the factory he was guarding through the wee small hours. He would be well set-up with a goodly supply of booze and studying form in the racing paper of the day. He certainly knew his 'gee-gees', as he affectionately referred to them.

Listening to him, he made a fortune. In reality he lost a fortune, albeit a small one.

'When his ship came in' he was going to give us all whatever we wanted. But none of us ever witnessed its arrival.

"Wonderful, wonderful to see you all again."

His eyes twinkled as his Irish brogue rumbled out, whilst filling Mother's newly whitewashed doorstep with his gargantuan frame. A lifetime of Guinness coursing through his veins had given him a blotchy red face and a barrel-like body that was kept in check with braces and the most enormous shiny, black leather belt – a semi-permanent appendage.

He pointed down to his familiar tatty old shopping bag, held with fingers that resembled pumped-up sausages.

"Guess what, children?" answering himself in the same breath.

"Kitten, I've got you all a kitten," he proudly announced.

He produced kittens like a musical hall magician pulling rabbits from a hat. They often shared his bag with a bara-brith loaf, spuds or a pint of milk. As kids, he seemed great fun but later my mother, bit by bit, introduced us to her real father and I began to realise that sadly he had been a far from perfect specimen of manhood.

His wife, Sarah Baker before marriage, by contrast was one of the most welcoming and gentle people I remember. Dumpy and cosy, with a weatherbeaten face that had seen plenty of life.

"Welcome, my dear little children," she greeted us whenever we went to see her in Newtown.

She would bend down and sweep up the smaller members of the family from the ground, securely tucking them under each arm like a mother swan and her young. To make ends meet, she ran a shop in a very small front room, in her small house, on the busy corner where Wellington and Henry Street met in the Newtown part of Chester.

"Follow me around the back of the counter and see what I can find you."

She was always so pleased to see us.

Almost falling over one another we scurried through a small gap. We were once again in a favourite spot of mine. A veritable Aladdin's cave. We showed little interest in scrubbing brushes, bread and soap. But we did in the big glass jars of mouth-watering, colourful sweets and soon Grandma was unscrewing the black tops to pour out a few goodies into our grubby, cupped hands.

Sadly, however, Granddad also took a shine to things around the counter. Especially the money in the till.

What with a husband taking with one hand and customers working on 'tick,' and "Oh to be sure, Mrs. Stanton, I'll give you a bit more tomorrow, all right…" profit was out of the question but at least some food was to hand most of the time.

She was a proper grandma. A big heart filling a big body. Perhaps it's what you might have expected from someone that had worked hard on the land when she was younger. I can only wonder what would have been if she'd married someone else. Her well-to-do farming parents, no doubt thought the same.

She deserved a lot better, not someone that constantly subjected her to tirade after tirade following hours of heavy boozing in the Durham Ox and Barley Mow pubs. It so often ended in her being physically abused.

The part of the city where they lived was stuffed full of row upon row of terraced housing. Dark dwellings with heavily lace-curtained windows and dismal black and brown doors that people suddenly disappeared behind or popped out from.

It must have been impossible to keep secrets from neighbours, to have privacy of any sort. After all, many of the houses, including my grandparents', shared outdoor privies and the smallest of yards, where cupboards with fine mesh doors made manly efforts to keep dairy products cool and nearly fresh.

Long streets, narrow streets, turning tight corners into more streets as far as the eye could see.

All going nowhere exciting.

The closeness of the buildings appeared to tug down the grey, grit-laden smoke that constantly poured from every tiny chimney pot, settling down among matchstick figures going about their lives.

Women, hair scragged together with rollers, old before their time, pushing prams with two or three urchins hanging on. Men, bent double, pushing bikes with wobbly wheels, loaded up with sacks of coal and wood, balanced precariously in the frame and on top of the handle-bars.

*

"Quiet, Grandma's speaking."

Respect for her was absolute. My other Grandma, my dad's mum, born Rose Ann Ashton.

We froze. Not a wasted word, and she knew the whereabouts of everyone around her. Her words had a strange stretched, echoing feel to them, starting at a high level to establish contact with the person she was talking to, tailing off quietly as the sentence continued.

Measles, then, could be so cruel. Weakened by it early in life, she eventually lost all sight and hearing in her forties. She looked so gaunt and fragile. One eye bulged out more than the other. With thin, rather sinewy arms and neck, severely drawn back greying hair and long pendant earrings dangling from somewhat elongated lobes, she had a classical Victorian look about her.

I remember hand-knitted grey clothes. Drab clothes, draped over most of her body. It was the only occasion that I have seen someone using the Braille system to read. She fascinated me as I wrote big letters on the palm of her hand with my tiny fingers.

K, E, N.

Of course she knew it was me, having done her homework by running highly-sensitised hands over my face as I settled down on her knee. Was this the same lady that magically entranced us whilst never sparing the rod with her own children?

It was.

"She could be a right tartar," my mother often reminded us. I say she was entitled to be, given what life had thrown at her.

And how did her husband, Charles Joseph, cope?

He was in charge and then again he wasn't. He was the man of the house, the breadwinner, doing all the manly tasks and many of the not-so-manly tasks that were the preserve of the wife in those days.

What, a man in the kitchen in the Forties and Fifties?

A man dusting! A man making beds! Whatever next?

But Granddad was big enough to take it in his stride. We all loved him. He was a super Granddad. He worked on the railways as a wagon repairer, was a useful carpenter and was often seen wheeling a wooden handcart around, with a pipe and baccy pouch always to hand.

When he married Rose Ann, he knew that eventually she would no longer be able to see and hear him or anyone else.

He wasn't much over five feet to start with and seemed to shrink significantly in his latter years. He had a wonderfully large hooked nose, which when he removed his dentures, could just about touch his equally proud upturned chin. We had our own real live Mr Punch!

They lived in Hoole, a suburb of Chester, less than a mile away from where my mother was brought up. An area not quite as heavily populated as Newtown but the dwellings were similar in size and nearly as gloomy. The uninspiring leaded amber and bottle-green glass in the front door failed in its attempt to allow light to pass through.

Darkness still prevailed on the turning of the front door knob and entering the long, thin hallway. My father often reminded us that much of his studying was done in the invariably freezing-cold outside loo in the backyard. With seven people in a small dwelling, it was the only place he found to 'get his head down to his books'. We half believed him. More importantly, it had the desired effect in bringing us to our senses when we were becoming restless in our comparatively warm and spacious house.

*

As was often the case in those days, daughters, or in particular the younger daughter, would be expected to stay put, looking after their parents till they passed away, propped up on a generous sea of pillows in the relative comfort of their own bed.

Well, a sort of comfort. I recall dark, pokey little bedrooms, dominated by enormous wooden beds with hardly room to walk round them.

Rosary beads dangling from the corner posts. Rosaries recited as and when a little help was needed from on high.

A dark wooden dresser whose sole job seemed to be to support a large white jug of water, sitting in an equally large white bowl, and a towel or two.

'Don't anyone touch that one. That's for Doctor so-and-so.'

It was a time when doctors were at the peak of their powers, which some used with arrogant impunity.

"Trust me, I'm a doctor."

"Don't question my judgment, I'm a doctor."

"Yes Doc, no Doc, three bags full Doc."

At floor level, chipped enamelled bedpans, always seemingly full to the gunnels, were constantly at risk from our busy little feet rushing to and fro.

Such visits to witness grandparents in their twilight years are etched vividly in my mind, and no doubt in those of my brother and sisters. And none so memory-tugging as the sound of the squat wooden clock on the sideboard, eerily chiming off the hours on the way to their final resting place.

On my dad's side of the family, his youngest sister Emma drew the short straw, remaining at Clare Avenue until her parents departed this world. And as if that was not enough, her gappy teeth and enlarged thyroid gland left her very exposed to the cruel kind of ridicule that only groups of young kids, like me and my siblings, could conjure up.

Whether such responsibility was thrust upon her or not, I never knew. Bad enough at the best of times, but with such a demanding mother, with her remaining faculties honed to perfection, she must have needed the qualities of a saint. Woe betide her if Grandma, on one of her regular sorties around the house, found an inkling of dust, or a shortfall of 'spit and polish' on that wonderful piece of engineering, the blackened cast-iron range, that boiled the kettle, heated the house, baked the bread and cooked the food.

And of course kept the cat warm.

Completing the surreal vision I have of the living room, was a caged yellow budgerigar, lurking incongruously in the shadows. Maybe it provided much-needed companionship for Aunt Emma.

Many a time the story has been told when my mother saw Aunt Emma approaching our house. Looking down the road through the fancy bay window, she muttered something under her breath that was not meant for our ears. Up to her eyes in work as usual, the last thing she wanted was another distraction. As the knocker sounded, my eldest sister Sheila raced to the door, struggling on tiptoes with the catch. Opening it eventually, she looked up at her Auntie, blurting out,

"Good God, Emma's coming."

Mother never told us how she got out of that one!

Aunt Emma grew to be as severe and strict as her mother. She married, but remained living with her parents. Husband Eric no doubt helped her retain some sanity. I liked Uncle Eric but didn't see an awful lot of him. He locked himself away in an upstairs room whenever we went visiting. Strange really, that this tall, handsome man, complete with a rakish moustache that he cultivated in the RAF, had trouble facing the outside world. Perhaps he felt that what privacy he had, in such a congested house, needed to be protected at all costs.

He was a fantastic model maker. Ships, cars and aeroplanes: you name it, he could make it. Just occasionally, my brother and I would manage to prise ourselves into his tiny room to steal a glimpse of his latest creation on the stocks. No doubt this hobby was an antidote to the nondescript boring job that I recall he had at the Northgate Brewery in Chester. We had great fun with his balsa and tissue paper creations that flew wonderfully, but in the hands of small lads their life expectancy was very short. Still, with more balsa, paper and glue they would soon be airborne again.

*

My dad's eldest sister, Rose, by contrast, had a charmed life. The only one in the family to get a place at a local grammar school and for that, she had plaudits and resentment thrown at her in equal amounts. She quickly found a man, married and emigrated to Canada. Her husband Frank got a job as a purser on the cruise liners plying their trade up the western seaboard from Vancouver to Alaska. The only contact ever made was at Christmas time when Auntie Rose would detail the wonderful scholastic achievements of her daughters, Sylvia and Rosalie, in very long boring airmail letters.

Such missives turned out to be the forerunners of the multiple letters that arrive today on my doorstep in ever increasing numbers, from friends and relatives alike. Who, apart from immediate family members really want to know what level Penelope has reached with her violin, how many GCSE 'A' grades dear old Johnny got last summer, and really, did Fiona reach the heady heights of milk monitor in only her first year? Perhaps it's one of my many quirky shortcomings, but I don't like to dwell on such achievements in my family and consequently, I'm afraid, these seasonal letters today quickly find their way to the waste-paper bin.

Recently, I saw cousin Rosalie after a gap of nearly fifty years. Bizarrely, there she was on the dockside in Vancouver as I arrived by ferry from the island, displaying a sign with my name on it. It wasn't needed. She was a clone of her mother and I could have picked her out from a crowd of ten thousand, let alone the three people that stood idly around waiting to greet passengers. Proof, if it was needed that, like it or not, we all grow to look like our parents.

*

Uncle Reg, my motor racing mentor, married Dad's middle sister Minnie. Dumpy and cuddly, she always made us feel welcome at her home in Great Boughton, a stone's throw away from the Shropshire Union Canal. Again, it was an area of row upon row of small terraced housing. Soulless-looking from the outside, but once through the tiny front door, we were quickly made at home with a plate of freshly-made cakes pushed beneath our noses. And dandelion and burdock in tumblers which we had fun with, precariously perching them on the arms of large, well-worn cosy chairs.

"Reg, Reg! No..."

Before Aunt Minnie could intervene, he was at it again.

"So who's the lucky bloke you're going out with, Sheila, at the moment?"

My big sister so hated the inevitable question from the smooth operating Uncle Reg every time we met up, that she started to blush before he'd hardly opened his mouth, knowing what was coming. The rest of us weren't much better at handling our rather inquisitive uncle as we approached that age where he thought we should be going about 'courting'.

Father had tried to steer us all down the road of learning at the expense of 'sap-rising' activities. Books, books and more books.

Perhaps he popped bromide in our drinks when we weren't looking? Maybe. Who knows. He was in charge.

"You'll have plenty of time to get up to that sort of malarkey when you've finished studying m'lad. Keep 'ed down now and you'll benefit in long run."

I occasionally wonder whose advice would have served me best – Dad's or Uncle Reg's.

*

The baby of my dad's family, Harry, had the most exciting job of them all during the war, navigating Wellington bombers whilst only in his early twenties. That took some beating and he was a particularly favourite uncle of mine. He didn't lecture, he listened and always showed a genuine interest in what I was up to. He married Betty, a publican's daughter from Preston and they settled to the west of Chester, close to the Welsh border in Saltney.

Venturing out to see them, normally on a Sunday afternoon, we would be welcomed by Aunt Betty pushing a trolley full of jangling spirit bottles. She'd ask Mother what she'd like and with a bit of diplomacy she would reply: "Well, Betty, a cuppa would be real nice at the moment."

*

The war messed up many careers and men being demobbed often had to radically rethink what they might do for the rest of their lives. And this at a time when we had a burgeoning population and jobs were hard to come by. So, it was often a case of taking what was on offer and hope it worked out.

Mind you, the 'old boy network' was alive and well and kicking. Being a member of the Freemason movement helped considerably. Now that was something to get my dad going.

"That damn lot. Scratch my back and I'll scratch yours."

"Brotherly love, faith, charity? That's all me eye and Peggy Martin."

"A load of hogwash."

"Those councillors in the Town Hall. They're all at it."

"And that damn Duke of Westminster. Does what he likes in the city."

On and on he chuntered on to anyone that was left in earshot.

Mind you, Father conveniently forgot that the Catholic Church he regularly attended had its own secretive society, in the form of the Knights of Saint Columba. Just as much greasing of palms took place in that outfit. Dad's memory wasn't too good at that point.

*

Doesn't every family have an Aunt Sally ? We had one. My mum's younger sister.

"Hello, Aunt Sally."

"D'you mind, 'Aunt Sarah' to you, Kenneth," when she was in posh mode and trying to put me in my place. "And I don't think you're very funny, taking the micky out of my friend Teresa Green."

"Well, what colour are they auntie, if they're not green," I used to cheekily answer back.

It was healthy banter Aunt Sally had with all her nephews and nieces. Two years younger than my mother, it fell to her to stay at home and look after Gran and Granddad Stanton, so she remained a spinster all her life. Family discussions as to why some daughters took on this rather unglamorous task never got very far. Mother would confirm from time to time that she had ample opportunities of marriage, and photos in her heyday suggest she was a fine, attractive lady, slim with fine features and lovely silvery hair.

I did get annoyed with my mother when she prattled on about her sister.

"Our Sally is always going on holiday, somewhere round the world. Here I am, stuck at home with you lot, creating nothing but trouble."

It was times like this that I let rip at my mother. She conveniently forgot about the pleasures and satisfaction in having children and a supportive husband. The older she got the more outspoken about her sister she became. But it wasn't all one way, Sally often went on about her big sister getting the best of this, that and the other.

"You know Kenneth, our Nell always took the best stockings and left me holey ones."

She reminded me again recently of such inequalities. Not after or before my mother's funeral, but during it! I can put it down to healthy rivalry and no hard feelings.

In middle age my aunt busied herself more and more in religious activities. With friends, she often visited the Holy Land and seemed to be a regular at the Vatican.

"D'you know, I was from here to there away... are you all listening – you're as bad as those girls in the factory... from here to there away from the Pope. I swear to God he smiled at me."

"Yes, yes, auntie."

Did she bore us silly.

"Her tongue is the nearest thing to perpetual motion I've ever come across," Father regularly reminded us.

As a regular silverware polisher at St Werburgh's church, we mischievously reckoned that she hoped Canon Murphy and the other priests would look leniently on her when handing out penances during Saturday morning confession sessions. I know only too well the feel of aching knees after tackling a goodly penalty of countless 'Our Fathers' and 'Hail Marys'.

She squeezed in pilgrimages to Lourdes when work permitted. Work was at Davies, a tobacco-packaging company in Canal Street, joining at fourteen straight from school. During her forty-five years she got to the lofty level of supervisor and often droned on, "Honest to God, you wouldn't believe what foul-mouthed young tarts I have to control in that place."

No doubt she gave as good as she got. We had glimpses of it from time to time when she whisked us away against our wills on dreaded coach trips to the seaside in North Wales and the Wirral. Out of earshot of my parents she introduced us to our first smutty jokes and somewhat risqué stories, laced with lavatorial humour.

I finished up in disgrace on such an excursion. To a four-year-old, the back of a shining, bald, pink pate had a certain attraction for a sand-encrusted spade that was my constant companion on such days out. Hardly had the poor bloke started to wipe away the blood, than my treasured possession was on its way out through the coach window.

"That'll teach you to behave," snarled my aunt, hoping at the same time that the injured party would be pacified. Silence and tears accompanied me the rest of the way home.

I'm sure we contrived to find disasters. Looking for trouble. That's it. Let's rock the boat. That's what it was all about when Aunt Sally tried to entertain us. We didn't want things to go swimmingly and smoothly, did we? How ungrateful we must have appeared.

Today, things are different. Very different. Now we have bestowed iconic status on her and no gathering is complete without the raising of a few 'Aunt Sally' moments. A mirth maker by default without equal for me and my cousins, but we wouldn't have been without her.

When she retired from the tobacco factory, all she had to show for devoting her entire working life to one company was a miserly pension. No carriage clock. No flowers, not even a tinny Timex wrist watch. She deserved more. A lot more.

*

Acting as an effective antidote to Aunt Sally, Mother had two level-headed brothers, Bill and Jim, who were happy to listen rather than chat all the time. Both were superb athletes and often competed in races where sizeable amounts of money were gambled. Stories circulated of them using pseudonyms to confuse punters, reaping relatively rich pickings in the process. Winning a grandfather clock on one occasion, they had to resort to cutting a hole in the canvas top of their battered Singer car, which had set their mother back the grand sum of £10, to bring it back home from Wales.

Uncle Bill, the third born after my mother and aunt, spent most of the war as a dispatch rider in Belgium, The Netherlands and Germany. On leave he would turn up with toys that lit up our eyes. Dolls that had double-jointed arms and legs, with eyes that opened and shut, small wooden cars and a mouth organ. After the war, he went back to work for the Shell oil company in Ellesmere Port, who had very generously kept his job open for him. He married May, a psychiatric nurse. She died of cancer in her late 30s, having travelled the length and breadth of the country in pursuit of a cure. Her young children, Pat and David, became like a sister and brother to us, as my mother opened our house to them whenever they needed it.

Uncle Jim, the youngest of the four, started his working life as an apprentice butcher but by the time he meant anything to me he was a policeman. During the war period he was part of the security force protecting the docks in Runcorn. A gentle giant of a man, we all loved him as he made us feel very comfortable in his presence. He married the beautiful Doreen and had five boys. Poor James died when he was only two.

Chapter 11

Junior School

By the time that I was ready for school, being the third of four children, a pattern for my early education had already been established by my elder siblings. Five was the age at which you went to school in the 1940s. It wasn't challenged, and parents weren't desperate to get their offspring into full-time education as soon as they were weaned off the bottle, thus allowing them a decent run at childhood before the straitjacket of formal education.

The first decision my parents had to make was between the local village school or the nearest Roman Catholic one in Chester, some three miles away. For convenience, the local one just down the lane, which specialised in nature walks, collecting newts, tadpoles and studying hedgerows and ploughed fields should have been the first choice. But already my father, who educated himself after he left school, was showing his desire to provide us with a level of education that many of his generation were deprived of. He also had to attempt to comply with the ruling of the church.

So it was off to St Werburgh's R.C. Primary School. Heaven knows why classes were mixed until seven, and thereafter segregated.

"The children from those Catholic schools, they are so well behaved aren't they?" was often heard in the neighbourhood. Little did outsiders realise the techniques employed by the staff to ensure that we did exactly what we were told. Discipline was achieved at a price. Without question.

Back then, teachers spoke and pupils listened. It was indeed a brave and adventurous child who engaged a teacher in conversation. Early on we got to know how discipline was achieved in the school.

The cane and the ruler!

The former for the backside and the latter, edge-on, across the back of the hand. Their use was almost as common as falling over in the playground. As with many memorable events early on in life, the magnitude and significance often cannot be put into their rightful context until much later. Understandable, I suppose, since the passage through life is largely about comparing and contrasting situations at different times.

Extreme as it might seem, there must have been a seriously sadistic element in many of my teachers. The fact that the same boys committed the same indiscretions time after time, meant that the severe corporal punishment being meted out was totally ineffective. There did not appear to be any attempt to 'get to the bottom of things'. No time for pupils to put their point of view. No parental involvement.

"You again, Barlow. Headmaster's study immediately."

That meant at least three whacks with the cane, for starters. More, I suspect, if the head was in a bad mood.

Little good could be said about my headmaster. He was tall, fat, bald, had a bright-red face and always seemed to wear a powder-blue suit. He put the fear of God up us all as he strutted the corridors, often with cane in hand, flexing it meaningfully as he approached you. The only time that parents saw him was at St Werburgh's Church on a Sunday morning. He stood before the altar, facing the congregation as they entered, making a mental note of who had and had not turned up. Fortunately, with devout parents, and bikes, we never failed to turn up on 'parade' every Sunday. Furthermore, we got plenty of 'brownie points' for going up 'en masse' to receive holy communion.

The punishment for missing Mass was evident on Monday morning as lines of lads formed up outside the Head's study. The regular excuses were trotted out but to no avail and the same backsides beaten hell out of, time and time again. With no Parent/Teacher Associations, no open days and no assemblies for parents, teachers could do what they wanted. And they did.

Kids rarely confided in their parents where corporal punishment was concerned. Teachers were always right and telling your mum or dad about some slight indiscretion you'd committed in the classroom, could mean a repeat dose of the same treatment in your own home.

I managed to avoid the cane but was not so lucky with the ruler.

It all started rather innocently.

White ceramic ink wells bunged up with blotting paper, dip pens, ink monitors and blue stains on every piece of classroom furniture. Now we were about to be introduced to the magic of the ink rubber. Not only could it remove ink, supposedly, but in the wrong hands it resulted in your exercise book looking as if it had been attacked by a family of mice. It was an arithmetic lesson and several times I tried to erase mistakes. Progress was painfully slow so I crossed them out with my pen and entered the correct figure above. Three times. It had always worked in the past. And it had worked this time, so I thought.

The teacher, doing his round of the class in imperious fashion, towering above us, started down my row. I could sense something was not right. He stopped near me. Perhaps he was admiring my new satchel. Perhaps not. Arithmetic was one of my favourite lessons, and I generally kept my head well above water, hovering around the top of the class. Without warning, the teacher yanked me out of my desk, marched me to the front of the room.

"This lesson is about rubbing out, not crossing out. Right hand boy. Hold it straight. Out properly, boy."

I realised what was coming because it had happened many times before. But never to me. My hand was the right way round, knuckles uppermost. With an air of satisfaction, he entered his desk, emerging with the weapon. A twelve inch long wooden ruler. No further words were exchanged. I received 'three of the best' with the sharp edge and was sent back to my desk. No tears then, but come the end of the lesson, in the playground, surrounded by my friends, out they came. Only those that have experienced it, know of the pain.

The only good that seemed to come from such an experience was a uniting of children, a bonding process in the face of adversity against unloving people masquerading as teachers. Of course there were some friendly teachers, but their acts of kindness and under-standing sadly are lost with the passage of time. Only the nerve-shat-tering occasions seem to be on the agenda when recalling memories of those junior school days.

Well, perhaps not quite. Some light relief was at hand when the weekly cattle market hit town. Held at Gorse stacks, it was only a short distance from the school. Sheep and cattle were herded through the narrow streets and it was not usual for them to stray into the open doors of houses or fall into the Shropshire Union Canal, causing general mayhem and giving us much to laugh about. At Christmas time, fowl was added to the list of the traders. But what I looked for-ward to mostly was seeing action in the blacksmith's at the top of George Street. The farmers would bring their horses in to be re-shod and if we had time before catching the bus home we would poke our nosy little heads into the smithy to catch a glimpse of the action. A roaring coke furnace, bright red hot metal being hammered this way and that, and lots of smoke from the horses' feet. It always fascinat-ed me that the horse just stood there, uncomplainingly. Whilst the market was going on, some of the farmers took advantage of their time away from the fields and paid a visit to Trickey's barber sbop in Frodsham Street, followed by a few pints in one of the many pubs in the area before returning to business.

I left St Werburgh's at ten and had twelve months at the junior part of the King's School before 'joining a big boys' school'.

Chapter 12

Senior School

The 11-Plus exam reeked havoc up and down the land. It was a crude and divisive tool to assess the ability of kids nervously feeling their way, with teachers that left a lot to be desired, many receiving their training 'on the job'. The rest of our lives depended upon the outcome. Pass, and doors opened easily. Fail, and you could spend the rest of your life explaining what went so wrong on that fateful day. I was fortunate to pass – probably a 'scrape-through' rather than a distinction. I never knew the details.

My parents also entered me for the King's School Entrance exam. Again I surprised many people, particularly my sisters, by being offered a place. On religious grounds I should have been heading 20 miles north, to St Anselm's in Birkenhead, the nearest Roman

Catholic Grammar School. But my parents deemed it too far to travel. So come September 1952, I started at the King's School in Chester, with the possibility of transferring to St Anselm's at 14.

In the event a deal was done. I stayed in Chester for all my secondary education. To make up the shortfall in R.C. dogma, which was hardly surprising, the school having been founded by Henry the Eighth, I had to attend the Ursuline Convent on a Monday evening for an hour of religious instruction with Mother Matthew. I had a one-to-one session with a lady covered in black and a starched white bib. A thin, pointed nose supporting her specs gave her an owl-like appearance and I can't say that the atmosphere ever rose above freezing. Light-hearted chat was definitely not on the agenda. It was an experience clearly etched in my memory.

With my ability to blush profusely at the mention of a female's name, timing was critical to minimise the contact with hundreds of girls fanning out from the school, over the pavements and narrow streets. Having a sister and cousin at the school seemed to make it worse. This was an unplanned form of punishment, in many ways worse than the cane or ruler. My parents were unaware of the possibility that their dear little lad could have been mentally scarred for life.

In the event, I weathered the storm, did three years under the nun's tutelage and then returned to normality. Despite Mother Matthew's efforts, her rather unusual male student was definitely not heading for a Seminary.

Starting secondary school, a battle on two fronts began. As I entered the den of great expectations, I was also exposing myself to the wrath of many children in the village and particularly their parents.

I lost my best mate, Jack. His mother, a Londoner living an uncomfortable life in the raw north, hated me simply because I was now at what she called 'a fancy school', whilst her son had gone to Overleigh Secondary Modern School. I was no longer welcome at their house even though we had been inseparable for many years. Birds nesting, trucking, biking, swimming in the local river Gowy, cricket, football. You name it, we did it. Always together. Fortunately, he passed the transfer exam at 13 to the Chester City Grammar School and he never looked back. Sadly the damage done by his mother meant that we went our separate ways and a wonderful friendship had foundered so sadly. It was a painful first step into the adult world, the start of the long process of growing up.

As events turned out, a lad from the Overleigh Secondary Modern School was to became one of my closest teenage mates. Sadly, Dave Teague died in a motorcycle accident at the tender age of 20, whilst training to become a policeman.

*

My school colours could hardly be considered subtle. Green, blue and white stripes adorned every piece of my uniform. That was bad enough. But uniforms purchased at different stores had noticeably different shades of green. Browns of Chester, famously founded in the reign of George III, had a shade of light green which announced itself with a statement of superiority. The presence of heavily dressed and decorated doormen meant that only the well-heeled entered Browns. Such people must have found money growing on trees.

On the other hand, the Etonian, and don't be swayed by the name, suppliers to the less well-off Cestrians, had a no-nonsense dark bottle green. So immediately in a playground filled with over 500 lads, you could instantly tell where the money was. Unless you were very poor and your parents had bought second-hand. Now, those lads had real problems!

On the buses, I had to withstand the inevitable slagging-off from the secondary school kids and was always being tested as to what I knew and more to the point, what I didn't know. Still, this period soon passed and at school I had to get used to being surrounded by the academic cream, collected up to 30 miles away from Chester. Boy, were there some eggheads! From being always near the top in my junior school, all of a sudden I was wallowing in the bottom half of the class, apart from maths, where I was of reasonable quality.

The staffroom was packed with ex-Oxbridge men, mostly with private means, who had gone into teaching, I suspect, because it was respectable and allowed them to venture onto the continent during the long summer months. They were amongst the early discoverers of mainland Europe. This was at a time when most of the people in these islands still headed for the not-so-bright lights of Blackpool, Brighton and Bognor.

The teachers had some wonderful material to play with. Bright lads, keen to learn, desperate to get to grips with Homer's *Iliad* and *Odyssey*, and other rivetting reads. At the opposite end of the spectrum, I was surrounded by lads more interested in reading sports magazines, the *Eagle* and *Hotspur*. Well, we needed light relief to rest our brains after the pounding they took attempting to decline Latin verbs and the like.

*

Eccentric. Superior. Godlike. Unapproachable. And the mandatory wearing of gowns completed the aura that they felt was needed to keep us undisciplined school kids in place. That sums up my teachers pretty well.

Our Headmaster was a member of the cloth.

He was in charge all through my years at the school. More than that: he was a permanent fixture when I arrived and remained so long after I had left.

He was feared by every boy at the school and I suspect by many of the staff as well. I have an image of him being in complete control. He talked slowly and quietly. We obeyed instantly. There were few brave lads who would engage him in conversation and the presence of his dog-collar hardly helped to bridge the gap.

Certainly not of Herculean stature, stripped of his gown and mortar board he wouldn't have stood out in a crowd. He took the occasional maths lesson, but contact time with him, thankfully for most of us, was minimal.

Our ancient school buildings, being part of Chester Cathedral, had enormously thick walls, dozens of exposed beams and leaded and stained glass windows that only allowed the passage of faint shafts of light and well-worn stone spiral staircases. Such surroundings elevated the headmaster to a monarch-like figure. His office at the end of the ground-floor corridor, towards the main entrance of the school, was a place to avoid. There was genuine concern for mates standing rigidly to attention outside the carved solid oak door. The stark light bulb hanging down from the high ceiling made little impression on the general gloom in the building. The laboured opening and closing of that ancient portal had a finality about it that made you rush by, for fear of being sucked in as another candidate for 'the executioner'. His faithful secretary, a thin bespectacled man, hovered in the shadows ready to move into action when his master clicked his fingers.

The Reverend was a regular user of the cane on errant lads. If the truth were known, there was probably much more to him than I ever witnessed. After all, armed with awards galore from Oxford, he no doubt had much to offer but little came my way. Or the way of most of my friends.

Along with a handful of other Catholics and two Jews, I was excused his daily address to the school at assembly time. The other lads somewhat envied us, and thought it a great achievement that we had extracted such a concession and had made a dent, albeit, a small one, in the tyrannical *modus operandi* existing at the school. Instead, we sat around in Room F, either finishing homework or playing shove-halfpenny on the baronial size windowsills. Occasionally we would get a call at the end of assembly.

"Bring 'em in to hear about the weekend's sporting achievements."

The Head's deputy was equally high in the discipline stakes.

Known to all as 'BT', he would have been equally at home in the Old Bailey, donning the black cap, before sending down another prisoner. He was a much smaller man than the head, barely reaching five feet, and squat with it. With the addition of a smartly clipped 'tash hanging on his upper lip and peering over the top of his specs, he put the fear of God into all. He was much more vocal than his boss.

'You guttersnipe boy,' was a wonderfully endearing term he often used. It was not perhaps not the sort of language you might expect from a Justice of the Peace, but that's how I remember him.

*

Wait a moment.

It was not all gloom and doom at the school. Some of the teachers were nearly human. Take 'Spid' Roberts, our physics teacher.

"Right, today boys, we are going to do some practical work."

But practicals were not quite practicals.

"Here you can see my collection of prisms, lenses, thermionic vacuum tubes and the fabled Van de Graaff generator. Look but don't touch. They are very fragile."

They all looked very nice sitting in their beautifully polished glass cabinets. But did we ever see action? Things working? Very rarely.

Mornings were best with Spid. After his regular visit to The Pied Bull for his liquid lunch, his productivity collapsed somewhat. And often he did, whilst scrawling on the board. Clutching at the desk to ease himself back into view, he constantly uttered, "It's the old war wound to my right leg again. Sorry, boys."

We always believed him. In fact most of us liked Spid. He rarely did us any harm and hardly dished out a detention. Afternoon periods were sort of do-it-yourself sessions. He regularly trotted out, "I've got some important marking to do, boys," as he limped off the raised stage that all teachers desks were mounted on. Into his small antiroom he went. We didn't have to wait long to witness smoke coming from around the cracks of the door. Eventually he returned towards the end of the lesson, asked how we had got on, set some homework and we moved on to the next subject. Amazingly, many of us did pretty well in physics at 'O' level.

We had a very well-heeled chemistry teacher, 'Gomer' Davies. Apparently he had done some ground-breaking research work whilst at Oxford but we never got to know the details. Turning up at our annual summer camp in North Wales in his British Racing Green XK120, Jaguar's latest sports car, he would politely introduce yet another 'sister'. He apparently had many 'sisters', who all looked so different.

As with physics, we saw little action in the chemistry laboratory. Occasionally we were introduced to litmus paper, test-tubes, bunsen burners, tripod stands and magnesium ribbon. Whether it was lack of enthusiasm on the part of 'Gomer', lack of money or on safety grounds that so little practical work was carried out, we could never fathom.

"What's your name, John Willy?" he would routinely ask each and everyone.

Only Mike Reidford, the class clown, had the nerve to answer "John Willy, sir."

And for that, he would spend the lesson outside the classroom on the landing. The rest of us enjoyed this regular attempt at humour.

Probably more interesting and certainly more approachable members of staff were those that had more modest academic achievements on their curriculum vitae. Mr Siddall from the local teachers' training college put the subject of geography over with great enthusiasm and it was one of the rare lessons where pupils fought to ask questions. You knew that you wouldn't be belittled, even by asking the most basic of questions.

The ever-smiling face of Tom Clamp, our ex-army physical training master was always welcome. But there again, he was taking us for a lesson that we all looked forward to, apart from poor old Dave Elston, who turned up in the changing rooms one day with his sister's hockey skirt. Relying on your mother to pack your school bag could be fraught with problems, not least a red face for weeks.

*

"Look out, Wilbers!" came the cry from near the back of the classroom. Too late. My head crashed down onto the desk lid. Apparently several minutes passed before some form of normality returned to my scrambled brain. 'Dick' Bentley, the senior geography master, had told me to stop talking a couple of times. An impudent 12-year-old disobeying him for the third time was too much. Colleagues later filled me in with the missing few minutes of my life. Without my knowing it, behind my back, the cloaked creature moved like a howling dervish. A trunk-like arm came powering down, ramming my head almost through the desk. Nothing more was said. I can't imagine what possessed me not to heed such warnings from a man whose reputation for toughness was legendary. Bentley had made his point. Quietness prevailed as the lads around the classroom took note not to be as foolish as 'poor old Wilbers'.

Solidly-built, balding, with an iron fist, there was something of an ageing SAS soldier about him.

"Of course I've swum across the Caspian Sea, boy. Winter time it was, breaking ice as I went."

Such comments established his authority early on with the new intake. His reluctance to accept help from a lifeboat, whilst sailing single-handed in a howling gale off Anglesey, added to his fearsome reputation.

"I was minding my own business – pity they couldn't mind theirs," was his bluff comment, reported in the national papers. He was a new hero for us, but we never let him know it. I often wondered what this genuinely tough guy got out of teaching geography to spotty adolescents that he could have eaten for breakfast.

*

'Johnny' Walsh was a different kettle of fish.

Full name: A. St G. Walsh, ex. Trinity Hall, Cambridge, teacher of scripture and mathematics.

He could have been born in Palestine, some 2000 years ago. Well, it didn't take much imagination to believe that this might have been a possibility. Here was a man of great wisdom with a heavily etched, studious face. He spoke in quiet measured tones. He had been wedded to the world of academia all his life and was now not far off retirement. There was definitely a strong feeling of a disciple about him with his heavily chalk-laden, moth-eaten gown adding to the image.

Not for him the world of physical violence to maintain law and order in the classroom. A few words was all it took.

"I have a simple system, boys, that you all need to know. It's 'TT, TT.' 'Talk in Test, Test in Tub.'"

Young kids appreciated brief, clear guidelines. This quietest of masters was brilliant at it and meant exactly what he said. The slightest hint of doing anything untoward in tests and exams, result-ed in a round O. And it was there for your parents to see at report time. Discussions were never entered into. He was perhaps the steel-iest of my teachers. Tough but fair and we respected him for it.

To misquote a metaphor, his 'words were mightier than the cane or a belt about the head'.

A lasting memory of 'Johnny' Walsh is of a small, hunched crea-ture, pottering down the gloomy corridors, carrying huge amounts of paperwork, faded sepia photos and dozens of tattered-edged maps of the Holy Land. Some wit called them 'Johnny's Dead Sea Scrolls'. It needed only a few followers for it to have become a truly biblical scene.

An avid train spotter, he was regularly to be seen at Chester General and Chester Northgate stations, complete with old rucksack, filling in Ian Allen railway books. More engines noted. Still more to go. A lifetime's activity, and one that I identified with for a short peri-od of my life during teenage years. Then I discovered the opposite sex to be more absorbing than seeing yet another 'Castle' class steaming into the city from North Wales. I often wondered what prompted such a very cerebral man to chase railway engines all his life, for he was still at it well into his twilight years.

*

Music and art were subjects that were never really taught in any depth. Some affinity was developed between the masters and those with natural talent or attending private music lessons. But for the bulk of us, we meandered along in an unstructured fashion. Crotchets, quavers, minims. Even now the words come to mind easi-ly, but I haven't a clue what they mean. Occasionally, we had to 'com-pose' a piece of music and Sutton, the Music master, would attempt to interpret it on his piano. He was such a nondescript person that I have difficulty in recalling any of his characteristics. He gave up with most of us from day one. My cause wasn't helped when my voice broke soon after I started the second year.

"Your voice, Wilbraham, is putting the rest of the class off from singing properly. It's the Growlers for you."

That meant private study, which was OK by me. Term by term, the Growlers grew in number, a by-product of the arrival of teenage years. Poor old Sutton must have become depressed to see class sizes dwindling as the years went by. It must have felt as though a bell had been placed around his neck, with onlookers bellowing 'unclean, unclean'. Still, he no doubt felt more comfortable with like-minded people around him, playing instruments and singing to a standard that he appreciated.

Whilst most of our lessons took place in the main school building attached to the Cathedral, we also used the building that once upon a time had been the Chester Blue Coat School. It was a short walk up Northgate Street, just outside the North Gate of the Roman walls. It was also adjacent to the Northgate Brewery, which spewed out the most disgusting stench when mashing and brewing were in progress. It could have put many a lad off beer for the rest of his life. Chemistry, physics and art were taught here. With the canteen also on site, finishing the morning session with one of these subjects had the added bonus of being able to get near the front of the dinner queue.

Yes, then, we called the midday meal dinner, followed by tea in the evening. Sometime later in life, dinner gave way to lunch and dinner took the place of tea. Tea became something that you took with crumpets when the vicar came round. In any event, such names were totally irrelevant at school. For growing lads, any form of food-time could not come quickly enough.

I suppose Orry, the art master, was the most sartorial dresser of all the staff. In view of the competition, this is faint praise indeed. Still, he made an effort to be different. A flamboyant moustache, RAF style, was constantly preened, and he twisted the ends as he bid you welcome and farewell.

"Right, get on with what you were doing last time," were his normal opening remarks. Occasionally he would actually teach. Like when we learnt about perspective.

Why perspective? Well it was about the only time that I can remember when he actually put chalk to board. A man of few words, and even less action.

Winter-time really brought the best out of him. Our art room was not the warmest place on the earth. In fact, on some days it seemed warmer outside. Collecting our work sheets, paints and pencils, we quietly continued where we had left off last time. Up front, Orry was prepared for anything that the elements could throw at him.

There was only one electric fire in the room. Nicely positioned to warm feet. His feet!

The camel-coloured duffel coat. No doubt a remnant from his art college days and still useful. A multi-coloured scarf, wrapped round his neck several times, completed the mummified look.

And finally, just to make doubly sure that hypothermia was not going to enter our room, our very caring art master had a flask of coffee at the ready. Ready for himself, which he sipped at frequent intervals. Meanwhile, his budding Picassos and Constables, suffering with the onset of frostbite, were struggling to hold pencils and paint brushes.

Still, as with music, these subjects gave us the opportunity to indulge in our dreams and rest our brains awhile, prior to the tougher challenges of Maths, English, Latin and Science.

*

On the sporting front, Robin Alden the rowing master developed quite a reputation for writing off boats with great regularity. His half-inch thick spectacles said it all.

"Come forward to row. Are you ready? Row."

Coxing the 1st Eight on the River Dee, he always insisted on bringing them back to the clubhouse from the Groves with a 'racing finish'. It was also the part of the river where day-trippers in their hired motor-boats pursued totally unpredictable courses. Lightweight, flimsy racing boats crumble like a well-baked biscuit on impact. It was a predictable event and the more ghoulish of us lined the towpath whenever Alden was in the area. He rarely disappointed.

I enjoyed all of the sporting activities at school, and generally made a presentable showing at most of them. Good, keen, but not outstanding. Being a late physical developer, still only five foot nothing at 16, I was in demand as a cox and had some success in a number of regattas with The Royal Chester Rowing Club. Cross-country running was also an event in which the smaller lads managed to get one over the larger boys. I put it down to greater stamina contained in a small frame compared to lanky lads where all their energies were going into reaching six feet and beyond.

My other modest success was in the boxing ring, where, representing my house in the annual event, I won two out of my three fights. Bloodied noses and crying mothers are still clear in my mind today.

When I was sixteen, I joined the School's Army Cadet Detachment.

Chapter 13

Playing at soldiers

"And the final announcement today," droned on the headmaster, "Anyone 16 or over can join the newly-formed Army Cadets."

It brought to an end the morning assembly. A buzz went around the hall. Quickly, boys' heads huddled together, and the inevitable, 'what d'you reckon. I'll join if you will,' and other reactions worked their way through the raucous gathering.

Joining the Army Cadets was to herald the start of another phase of my life. It was another watershed on my way to adulthood. Up to now discipline had been largely influenced by my parents and teachers. Now I was being thrown together with boys from a wider cross-section of society and regular soldiers. Competing against and co-operating with. Time for rough corners to be taken off.

The choice to join the Cadets was entirely mine. I must have felt ready for a new challenge. While many of my schoolmates shied away from the idea, some 25 of us chose to join with very few, if any, regretting their decision. I could have been comfortable with a career in the army should I have made that longterm choice.

We paraded after school on Friday evenings at the Drill Hall in Chester. A bold, castellated front to the building hid a spartan, heavily white-washed hall that we grew to know as a second home for two years. As part of the Cheshire Regiment, we joined forces with other detachments from the Chester Grammar School and Hoole, a small suburb to the east of the city. We were 52 Detachment and very proud of it.

They were exciting times. It was probably the first time in my life that I was seriously pretending to act out another person. And no hint of embarrassment as I was surrounded by mates doing exactly the same.

'Private Wilbraham' – I liked that.

"See yer later," we screamed to one another as we hurtled down the stone spiral staircases, across the coke-strewn school yard and onto our bikes in double quick time. We couldn't get home quickly enough on Fridays to get ready for parade.

The night before I had blanco-ed my gaiters and belt and now they were dry and ready to be finished. Great amounts of energy went into polishing the brass buckles and hat badge with Brasso, that ubiquitous product found in every household.

Bits of brown paper were carefully placed to mask the newly blanco-ed parts. Plastic badges were bought by some of the cadets, to cut down on the amount of elbow grease required. I considered it cheating.

My father added the occasional useful comment.

"Don't just do the bits that show lad – clean around back as well."

Boots received very special attention. They were the focal point in a kit inspection. Achieving ultra shiny toecaps and shin guards required hours of dedication. With the handle end of a spoon, spittle and lavish amounts of melted Cherry Blossom boot polish, a finish could eventually be produced with reflective power on par with a mirror. There was unbelievable competition to produce the best.

The only time I wielded the family steam iron was to press my uniform. It took me hours getting it just right. My mother must have thought it rather odd. She often suggested that I could expand my talents into other areas of clothing. But I never did. That was her domain!

"Eh, fancy 'aving to rely on 'em in times of war."

I could only guess at what was passing through the heads of passers-by on our way through the streets of Chester, heading for the Drill Hall. Some of the smaller lads had trouble filling their jackets, with material flowing well over their belts, whilst beanpole types looked as if they would snap in two if they were threatened with having to carry a rifle. Berets were worn at a variety of rakish angles.

"Fall in!" bellowed our Commanding Officer, Lieutenant Midgley, as he tried to bring some semblance of order to a babbling mass of teenage boys. Weekly inspection time.

Our detachment generally put up a presentable show. The boys from Hoole, however, could always be relied upon to bring words of 'advice' from the Commanding Officer.

"Bin dragged through a hedge backwards, eh, laddy?" or "Run out of blanco, again, eh?" were comments used with great regularity and never ceased in producing a muted titter among those gathered.

Arms drill, map-reading, camouflage, finding the enemy, rifle cleaning were covered in lectures, and from time to time, cadets were selected to impart their knowledge. Now that was something that made us all pay attention.

*

Being dismissed of our soldiering duties at 2100 hours, we promptly made a beeline for the 'Espresso' café in St Werburgh Street, nestling cosily in the shadow of Chester Cathedral. The billowing smoky blue haze from the coffee roaster discharging through a metal grille high up, sucked us in. Interlaced with jazz numbers, Elvis constantly pounded out his stuff, exercising his lungs on a glistening jukebox in the far corner.

Street cred had arrived at the 'Espresso' in the form of new tables covered in brightly coloured gingham and canvas-covered shiny tubular metal chairs. Naked bulbs were nowhere to be seen. Subdued lighting was now the order of the day.

This was the place to be, so we thought, on a Friday night. Bagging our places with casually thrown berets across the room, we formed a queue of sorts in front of a polished steel box that eerily erupted into life every now and again as black and white clad waitresses, turning a small wheel, injected steam into a never-ending row of cups.

Frothy coffee. That's what we ordered because it was about the only thing on sale. We huddled in small groups. While drinking, our eyes roamed. Looking for familiar faces. Girls that we normally dismissed out of hand in their prim and proper school dresses posed other challenges when turned out as painted dolls with well-filled tight sweaters and short skirts revealing desirable lengths of leg. They occasionally wore expressions of mild amusement. Most of us wished for more. That had to wait until Saturday nights at Quaintways and Clemence's dance halls.

Animated discussions broke out amongst the jazz freaks in our ranks.

"Saw you in Rushworth and Draper's last week."

"Yer, modern jazz I was thumbing through."

"Got good selection."

"What like?"

"Like Stan Getz, Thelonius Monk, Gerry Mulligan, Miles Davis, Brubeck."

The Trad Jazz followers aired their dissenting thoughts but were invariably argued out of court by the more cerebral Modern aficionados who were attempting to set their own style and break away from the commercial rat race.

The odd Mannikin cigar, increasing the intoxicating atmosphere, gave the place a continental flavour, though God knows why we thought this because none of us had ever ventured across the English Channel. Must have been based upon fertile imaginations and visits to the 'flicks'.

Most of us travelled by bike, discreetly hiding our trusty steeds away around the back of the café. But not so the Alexander brothers. They had a dad rich enough to buy them a Triumph Tiger Cub motorbike. Now that had to be parked right outside the café. £2000 a year in the late 1950s constituted being well-off and that, according to his sons, is what Mr. Alexander was on. In any event they were popular lads and handled their somewhat elevated status with style – we even got to ride pillion occasionally.

*

The real action-packed army activities took place, not at the Drill Hall, but at the summer camps, the shooting ranges and the nearby hills where we spent weekends crawling around on our knees, deep in mud, cold and not infrequently lost. The technical term was 'manoeuvres'.

For these activities we joined up with regular soldiers. They were real soldiers and they had a habit of letting us know what they thought of us spotty-faced school kids. I well recall the first summer camp that I attended in Ramsey, in the Isle of Man. There must have been around a thousand cadets from many parts of the mainland. For the first few days we could do nothing right. The battle-hardened Sergeant Major, lacing his sentences regularly with the 'f' word, had me trembling in my boots. Lateness, sloppy marching, untidy lines, failed kit inspection and so on. Then miraculously, light at the end of the tunnel as the week progressed. Less of the 'f' word and the hint of some praise began to surface. It is, of course, a well-used army technique to let you know just who is in charge and what you can expect if you have a difference of opinion with the Sergeant Major.

By comparison, our Lieutenant Midgley appeared a likeable wimp. He probably would not have made officer status in the Regular army but was happy with the limited power his position gave him in controlling a group of cadets. That first camp was particularly memorable and must have made our Commanding Officer a proud soldier. Our school detachment took just about every bit of silverware going, culminating with a victory in an all-night battle, enacted on a hill outside the town of Ramsey. How the other detachments must have hated us!

Weekends in the summer, out on the firing ranges at Sealand and

Altcar, gave us a special buzz. We were entrusted with serious fire-arms, the 303 and Bren gun, equipment capable of killing at 1,000 yards or more.

"Listen you lot. Very carefully. I will tell you once and only once," boomed the regular NCO in charge of us. We were all ears at the briefing session. Apart from their killing potential, hold them incorrectly and you could be visiting the hospital with a dislocated shoulder.

The days were long and we took it in turn to either fire or handle the marker posts from the butts, positioned immediately below the targets. Bullets landing short added to the occasion, spraying soil everywhere.

The journey home in our 5-ton, canvas-covered army lorry was always a time of great merriment and singing as we released the pent-up tension of the day. Yes, we were ready to defend our island if need be!

Chapter 14

Love at first sight, sound and smell

"You've got your Uncle Reg to thank for it," Mother regularly reminded me.

My fourteenth birthday was just round the corner.

Stuck with two sons who didn't have the passion of their father for motor racing, he scouted round for a member of the extended family to share his excitement for what Mother constantly described as "watching silly dangerous things going round and round, making far too much noise".

He drove an old black 1930s Morris, and when not using it to flog and maintain lawnmowers, it regularly found its way to public houses and his local bowling green.

Then, as if by magic one day, there it was. Parked outside our house. Short and barrel-chested, Uncle Reg swaggered up the pathway.

Sports coat, cravat. With slicked-back hair, he looked as if he'd just walked out of a Brylcreem advert. A regular playboy, given a chance, I dare say. Plenty of style but not a lot of money.

"There's a crackin' good racing car meeting coming up at Oulton Park next week, Ken. The British Empire Trophy. Fancy coming? Lots of big names."

As he spoke, between measured drags on a fag, his sparkling eyes flashed towards Mother, knowing her approval was needed. Charming people came naturally to him and of course he succeeded once again.

He must have done his homework. Knowing my weakness for all things mechanical, he was on to a winner.

The day couldn't come quickly enough. Hardly had his car stopped backing down the drive, than I was loading up. Unbeknown to me, I was embarking upon a ritual that would dominate much of my life.

Mother, even getting a bit excited herself, made sure that I had plenty of sandwiches, fruit and drink, and they were all firmly stuffed into an old army backpack. Waterproofs in the form of a bright yellow cycle-cape, sou'wester hat and a collapsible seat completed the shopping list.

"And take another jumper, Kenneth, in case wind gets up," was Mother's parting shot.

*

The race circuit was about a half-hour drive away and on the approach we were met by high-pitched whining of racing engines shattering the tranquil air of a wonderfully rural part of Cheshire.

"Doing some last-minute practice," said Uncle Reg knowledgeably.

I wound the window down to bring the cars even nearer.

The air was full of the smell of burning oil. Castrol R – a smell that still makes racing aficionados go weak at the knees. I had read about it. Now too, I was getting my 'fix'.

Excitement level had gone off the scale. And still, no sign of a car! As was typical in those days, traffic was relatively light and soon we'd parked in the outfield on the approach to Knicker Brook, one of the fastest parts of the circuit.

The action on the track by now had stopped for lunch.

We joined the trickle of spectators heading towards the paddock, via Clay Hill and the Dunlop Bridge. People, largely men of course, in groups of twos and threes, criss-crossed our path. Brogues, shooting sticks, flat hats and blazers hinted that wealth was alive and kicking in this part of the country.

Tension abounded and yet people appeared calm and spoke in hushed tones.

There was no great noise now that the racing beasts had been silenced and put to rest for a short while.

The tannoy system, in a matter-of-fact way, was busily giving out information as to who had withdrawn and which reserves had been accepted for the afternoon programme.

Our access to the paddock was unhindered. Mechanics were methodically going about their business; bonnets were open, spark plugs being changed, oil draining from sumps, petrol being poured. Occasionally I witnessed more frenzied activity as men in overalls disappeared beneath their cars, emerging oil-soaked, clutching pistons, con-rods and the like. Plenty of work to be done with precious little time to do it in.

I could identify with such activity as I had done something similar at home under the tutelage of my father on the family car. Scrutineering of cars arriving late was still taking place. It was a more relaxed exercise than it is today, where a millimetre in the wrong place can lead to disqualification. Then, as long as it looked right, it was given the all-clear.

I can't recall any particular desire to seek out the racing drivers themselves, in fact they were not that obvious. Often, they could be mistaken for mechanics and many were mechanics-cum-drivers. It was a far cry from the prima donnas of today, dripping with commercial endorsements and followed by scantily-clad bimbos and the designer-clad masses, wielding cameras and recording equipment.

"Hey, Uncle Reg. Him in that dark blue duffel coat, sitting on the side of that racer."

"Yer, barely out of school, if you ask me. Must have rich parents or someone thinks highly of him to let him loose with that beauty."

"He looks awfully young to be doing this death-defying stuff," I thought.

Other drivers looked like the well-to-do man about town, sporting slacks, shirts, dickie-bows and suede shoes.

Not unlike my Uncle Reg, on reflection.

*

On that first visit I was too overawed to approach the drivers with the race programme or a scrap of paper for their autographs. But those that did ask were happily dealt with, even by the big names of the day.

With races commonly about an hour or less in duration, the pits were not an area of great activity as they are today. Then, they were very basic in nature, providing a raised, flat surface some two to three feet wide, where a few people would assemble when the race got under way.

A clipboard and a couple of stop watches were all that was needed. Occasionally, a spare wheel or two, a petrol container looking like a milk churn and a funnel would be present. There was little concern for safety with every other person nonchalantly smoking as we sauntered around, absorbing the atmosphere.

Without warning, an ear-splitting roar erupted just behind me. Others soon followed, filling the air with a great cacophony of sound. It was music to my ears, but I dare say not to farmers living nearby the track.

"Come on, Ken. They're warming up for the first heat. Let's get back and sort out a place to watch from," said my uncle.

Half walking, half running we covered the ground quickly. Remembering that this was my first motor race, my highly excited state was to be expected.

The unknown, the noise, the smell, the crowds. Possible incidents as car jostled car on the limit of adhesion.

Hardly had we settled down on our collapsible seats by the entry to a very fast corner at the end of the Knicker Brook straight than the cars were on their way doing a warming-up lap.

It was a sports car meeting and entries were divided into three classes, depending upon engine size. The successful cars in each class then went forward to contest the final later in the afternoon. To eliminate the advantage of engine size, a handicap system was used, allowing all cars irrespective of size the opportunity to win outright.

The first heat was relatively uneventful.

A driver in heat two caught my eye. Running well up with the leaders he seemed to be nonchalantly caressing his trusty steed through the bends as if he was out for a Sunday afternoon stroll.

"Goin' faster than you think, Ken," said Uncle Reg, again knowledgeably.

"I know that," I thought, already becoming a bit of an expert at these things.

I recognised the driver's face and helmet.

The third heat was run in torrential rain and was won by a very experienced driver from France driving a factory-supported Ferrari. A serious incident, involving three Jaguars, took place yards away from me, the cars ploughing into a commentator's box in the process.

Come the final, the rain continued to skewer down, peppering the track and turning it virtually into a river. A few cars withdrew for a variety of reasons, leaving a disabled driver the winner.

Archie Scott-Brown.

He walked away with the princely sum of £250 for his weekend work. He would go on to win a number of international races despite only having a right hand. His withered left hand was attached to the steering wheel with a meaty-looking hook. Sadly he was to die racing, as so many of his contemporaries did during the next two decades.

A long day was coming to an end. Soon the car heater was breathing life back into my cold, weather-beaten body. I had no doubt at all that I would be back.

I discovered I had witnessed death only yards away.

At the time, few details were transmitted over the Tannoy system. A group of officials had been heavily hit by an out-of-control heavy piece of metal. The gravity of the situation was obvious to me and others around.

As is always the case in motor racing, serious accidents are reported very briefly, and 'death' is a word never uttered during a race meeting. It was next day that I heard that a course doctor had been killed and others very seriously injured.

That incident, as might be expected, is still clearly etched in my memory to this day.

However, what was not expected was the moving experience of being spirited into the cockpits of brave men, pushing their racing thoroughbreds to the limit.

I determined then, that one day, it would not remain just a dream.

*

Great drivers quickly learnt their limitations.

Many drivers didn't and many drivers died.

If I had gone to my first race meeting at the age I am today, rather than at thirteen, I doubt that I would have returned. But being youthful and impressionable, I did. Time and time again.

With mates, we would cycle the 12 miles from home and a kindly farmer near Esso Bend would let us dump our trusty steeds in his yard and then help us shin over the wall. I recall slipping him a small part of my pocket money. He seemed happy. We were even happier. The blokes on the turnstiles less so.

Much pleasure has been derived and many friendships developed over more than forty years by, re-quoting Mother, "watching silly dangerous things going round and round, making far too much noise."

I also became totally absorbed with a driver still doing his apprenticeship. Little did I know, or anyone else know, that he would prove to be one of the most naturally talented Grand Prix drivers of all time.

Perhaps I was also dreaming for him.

In the meantime, Tony Brooks had to spend another year on his text books at Manchester University if he was to qualify as a dentist.

Chapter 15

A quiet man with pulling power

He was just turned 23, some ten years older than me, when I first saw him in action at the Oulton Park motor racing circuit. He contested another couple of meetings that year at my home circuit in Cheshire. I also followed his progress at other circuits through the press and magazines.

I was so fortunate in catching him as he was embarking upon the difficult and dangerous task of graduating from Club and National events to those with a continental flavour. International events.

It was also the time that people in 'high places' were beginning to realise that this thin, slightly stooping figure, of average height, his light brown hair already receding, had more than his fair share of talent for conducting a car around a race track near to its limit of performance, with seemingly little effort.

No histrionics at the wheel for this man. No jutting out of the chin. No elbows in the air. Just an air of calm authority oozed from the cockpit.

His demeanour out of the car was similar. Quiet and dignified. Shuffling around in a heavily-toggled dark blue duffel-coat, elasticated-bottomed trousers and shoes that looked more like carpet slippers, he would acknowledge the presence of people as they passed by with a slight lifting of the head.

He was a student after all. But a well-behaved one.

Heaven knows what was going on inside. But externally, the innocent, slightly embarrassed appearance added to the mystery of this man. He didn't have to succeed in racing. Dentistry would do very nicely as a back-stop. Maybe it was this second string to his bow that set him aside from his peers. If he came a cropper on the track all was not lost.

Many of his fellow racers were already household names: Stirling Moss, Peter Collins and Mike Hawthorn. Larger than life characters, all they lived for was racing, happily indulging in many of the vices that were expected of men pursuing probably the most macho and dangerous of all sports at that time.

Drink, tobacco, women, late nights and so on. No doubt these 'pastimes' were in some way the antidote to living life on a very precarious edge.

But it wasn't for Brooks. Or, at least, I don't believe it was.

It was a time that death lurked on every corner of every race track. Not for those drivers the luxury of sand-traps, Armco barriers and the like that prevail today.

Leaving the comparative safety of the metalled track meant at best, a severe bruising of the body and in many, many cases, death.

It was also a time for the emergence of the professional racing driver. Gentlemen's agreements were giving way to legally drawn-up contracts. How was this going to affect my hero?

Which would come out on top – dentistry or motor racing?

*

I can only surmise that life at home must have been pretty comfortable. The first car that he went racing in was his mother's – a street-legal Healey Silverstone. He would drive it to race meetings, take part in the day's proceedings and then with his father back on board, head home to Manchester.

Even in those early days, he had an innate respect for the track, machine and no doubt his own skin. Severely damaging or writing off his car posed transportation problems in getting home – not to mention facing his mother with a plausible explanation.

I did not witness his first three years, but reading about his performances he clearly showed an exceptional talent emerging, steadily moving to more powerful cars as his experience increased.

It was all too easy to thrash around a race circuit as many did, in a somewhat flamboyant fashion, trying to attract attention. Such a style looked spectacular and often resulted in success. But it was generally patchy success. An occasional win, mixed with many a broken motor and plenty of accidents to boot.

Many a world champion and other top-line drivers eventually succumbed when their luck ran out.

Watching in those days, it soon became apparent who pushed their luck and who had sufficient respect, and fear, for what they were doing. Risk-taking is an inevitable part of motor racing.

Always has been.

Always will be.

The truly talented driver knows how far to go down that road. Of course there are factors beyond the control of a driver, the main ones being mechanical malfunction or design shortcomings. Even here, however, the astute driver can often feel the onset of a problem and slow or stop if he considers that the risk in continuing is not worth taking.

Brooks had more of these qualities than many of his fellow racers. In his whole career, spanning some ten years, he had only two very serious accidents. Both were largely outside his control.

He did however have those strokes of good fortune which ensured that the outcomes were not tragic, although looking at the cars afterwards, it was easy to think otherwise.

So I was witnessing a significant transformation in the life of Tony Brooks. The racing driver rather than the student.

Already in 1955, Aston Martin, a major player in motor sport, had seen fit to give him a couple of drives in their works-sponsored sports cars. Unfortunately, mechanical defects had prematurely ended both races.

Now as the season was beginning to come to an end, he was contacted by Connaught. At the time they were producing middle-of-the-road Grand Prix racing cars, without any particular success.

This offer was to change the face of racing both in the UK and much further afield.

"We have entered a couple of cars in the Syracuse Grand Prix, in Sicily. The beginning of October. Fancy driving one of them?"

A not untypical approach in those days when looking for a driver.

No doubt his reply ran along such lines, "Well, I was planning to put in some extra effort for my dentistry finals which will be coming up shortly. Still, if I take my books with me..."

And so started a life-changing venture.

Brooks would be going to Sicily to take on the might of the Italians on their own soil. The formidable Maserati team had entered four cars, to be driven by some of the top drivers of the day. They knew the circuit very well – it was on their back doorstep.

What was this unknown, young English man doing there? After all, he hadn't even sat in a Grand Prix car before, let alone driven one. It almost bordered on the farcical.

But, eh, all was not lost. He hopped onto a Vespa to get his first taste of the circuit. Then there was a practice period. Perhaps a couple of hours to get used to the car. If you're a fast learner that should be enough.

It was not long before the Italians realised that they had someone special in their midst. Brooks was a fast learner. Steadily, his practice times came down and down and further down.

The Maserati team management couldn't believe it and eventually sent their drivers back out to put this lad in his place.

Finally, practice was over. Brooks found himself in third place on the front row of the grid, having split the Maserati team down the middle.

"Still we will show him tomorrow what real Grand Prix racing is all about," was the general feeling in the Maserati camp. And no doubt 99 per cent of the crowd agreed. He hadn't handled these ultimate racing beasts in the heat of battle before. Now he was taking on several men with Grand Prix experience stretching back a decade or more.

The result was inevitable.

Or was it?

Come race day, the Italian crowd sat back to watch the procession, or so they thought.

Fighting with his first Grand Prix start, Brooks was left behind on the grid but gradually his machine burst into action and soon he was in hot pursuit of the pack ahead of him. To the consternation of the crowd, when they reappeared at the end of the first lap, there he was lying fourth.

He had no right to be there, thought everyone except Brooks himself and the small handful of English supporters, including the Connaught mechanics.

By lap four he was third and right behind the leader by lap eight. On lap fifteen he had passed Luigi Musso and was leading in his very first Grand Prix.

Bar for one lap, he showed the green tail of his Connaught to the complete field for the rest of the afternoon.

After nearly two and a half hours of avoiding the concrete walls that lined this tough, demanding Sicilian road circuit he finally took the chequered flag.

Just to rub salt into the wound, he broke the lap record by a mile.

Not only had Brooks won his first Grand Prix race but it was the first victory by a British driver at the wheel of a British car and in a continental Grand Prix since the days of Sir Henry Seagrave some thirty-one years earlier.

Fearing that the Italian newspapers would never believe it possible for the whole of the Maserati team to be beaten by an unknown car and driver, the engine was stripped and measured to ensure that it complied with the regulations.

That all was legitimate only rubbed in their defeat even more.

Boy's Own could not have bettered this!

*

In a relatively short space of time in 1955, I saw my first motor race and became engrossed in witnessing the rare talent of a local dental student-cum racing driver. In a few brief months, he bridged the gap between saloon and sports-car racing and his first Grand Prix with consummate ease.

He was to go on to many more greater feats but the romance of that year, seeing him emerge from relative obscurity to the international scene, was a very special experience.

Ask the man in the street about Brooks, you get the reply, "Tony who?"

Ask people who reached the very pinnacle of the sport and eminent seasoned commentators, they will give you a knowing look that he was up there with a handful of the very best, particularly where precision driving at high speed was at a premium.

He came very close on a number of occasions to becoming motor racing's Grand Prix World Champion.

Yes, it would have been a fitting climax for such a gifted driver. But if there was ever a driver that didn't really need such an accolade being bestowed upon him, it was Brooks. He was big enough not to need the support of such accoutrements about him.

And in any case, he might have become too famous and lost that special appeal he had for me. Perhaps selfishly, I didn't really want too many people to find out about my hero.

A genuine unsung hero if ever there was.

To this day, this most understated and gentle man conducts himself in the same manner as in his heyday on the racing circuit. His home is largely devoid of mementoes of yesteryear.

He is living proof that his dice with death over ten years had ended happily.

The no-go zone was clearly etched in his mind. Having a wonderful Italian wife and eventually five children no doubt convinced him that he had withdrawn from motor racing at the right time.

Chapter 16

Rubbing shoulders with Nature

"That's not fair, those conkers are enormous. Where d'you get 'em from?" enquired my mate Jack as he pushed open our back door and saw me drilling away with a meat skewer.

"Found a new tree the other day whilst I was out playing in one of farmer Dandy's fields, far side of the railway track," I replied rather smugly.

"Should easily make double figures with one of 'em, perhaps even become a fiftyer, if you pickle them," Jack added.

"Even better if I was to glue a metal nut inside," I replied, too busy to look up.

"Last year's 'laggies' will sort you out," butted in my older brother.

I agreed that those old gnarled dried-out blighters might pose a problem but not many lads had them.

Such was the seriousness that surrounded conker time.

Twisted strings, bruised knuckles and flying shrapnel added to the plot.

It was a time of the year that I felt clearly marked the end of long hot sunny days. To be replaced with magical mists hanging over the fields, dewy grass, gusting winds tearing the last of the stubborn leaves away from trees, laying a rustling, rich red-brown and yellow carpet upon the earth.

Welcoming gas street lights beckoned us home from school.

"Winter draws on," predictably announced my father every year.

A time to ready ourselves for the bleak times ahead I felt.

A time of plenty before winter shuts down mother earth for a rest.

But for now there was a lot to be done.

Things to pick, things to collect, things to eat, things to keep,

The heaving branches of fruit trees had to be relieved of their booty. Apples, pears, plums, damsons were crying out to be picked. A plentiful supply of fruit in our own garden didn't prevent my joining up with mates in scrumping sorties.

Not a bit of it.

Gardens bordering Porters Hill offered juicy plums, whilst Blackburn's enormous orchard hardly missed the pears and apples that we plundered on a regular basis.

Stomach-ache was not uncommon as we worked our way bravely through rock hard fruit on many occasions. My mother knew exactly what I had been up to and it generally resulted in a severe telling-off and a dose of foul milk of magnesia.

"Like drinking chalk," I would complain.

*

Saturday mornings heralded mushrooming. Around eight o'clock a group of us would casually gather together outside my house and set off across the fields. A veritable search party. Contact by whistling would help the latecomers to join up with us.

We all had our favourite spots and began fanning out by the time we reached the third field north of my house.

123

"I'm heading for where the railtracks cross one another," I shouted to my brother.

"OK, but watch the pond there, it's deep," he replied.

"Come on, Jack – those large oaks over to the right, that's where we'll strike lucky. Lots of horse muck, long grass and shade. Perfect conditions for mushies," I added.

Although their season lasted barely a month, these prized 'platers' were well worth waiting for. Having filled our hands with all we could carry, soon we were heading home to indulge ourselves in a monumental fry-up.

They were memorable meals and I never recall any ill-effects. We seemed to develop a sixth sense as to what was edible and what was not. Nowadays my family are not so convinced and I'm left to eat in splendid isolation what rich pickings I find on the roadsides.

I was not too keen on my parents' 'jam making' walks for elderberries, blackberries, hips and haws. They fostered in us the idea that family walks after Sunday lunch were, as we would say today, 'an opportunity for bonding.'

So what better way of harnessing six pairs of hands than in the autumnal activity of picking!

Suffice to say that my siblings and myself were sidetracked into other things: finding suitable bits of wood for catapults, bows and arrows, collecting wild flowers, leaves and nuts for school projects and so on. We noted fallen and rotten trees for future logging activities to see us through the forthcoming winter.

When the light began to fade, shadows lengthened and stomachs rumbled, it was time to give up on the hedgerows and return home to a roaring fire, where all four of us kids frantically beavered away for several more hours to finish our weekend homework.

Stuff of nightmares were those Sunday evenings!

*

With winter increasingly taking a stranglehold on life in the village, outdoor pursuits were confined largely to weekends.

Sub-zero temperatures brought the icing-over of shallow water collecting in the low surrounding fields. Strips of ice no longer than the length of a cricket pitch began to form. An ice rink had arrived on our doorstep.

But no popcorns, no ice-cream seller, no hot-dog stand, no musak. And certainly no sign of a designer label. Unless you viewed Dunlop wellies as a forerunner in the fashion stakes.

We were surrounded by hard-baked, roughly ploughed white fields and sparkling white hedges as far as the eyes could see. There was a feeling of isolation, an eerie silence akin to being in a polar circle.

We slid along on what ever part of the body hit the ice first. Time to talk, time to tease, time to make new friends. Simple entertainment at its most basic.

The ponds took somewhat longer to form ice sufficiently strong enough to hold us. Often we waited for the Evelyn Moorcroft test.

"If it can take 'Fatty' Moorcroft – what we waiting for?" said Ted Littler rather laconically.

Poor Evelyn. She was often seen up to her midriff in freezing cold water, making her way back to the bank to extract herself from the slimy, swampy primordial soup that lay at the bottom of our ponds.

She wasn't alone and most of us experienced that savage tug of the throat as we breathlessly crashed through the ice. Silence followed whilst the victim extracted themselves from the pond and hurried home, uttering beneath a suitably bowed head,

"See yer all later somewhere."

It was time to move on to another pond, in search of thicker ice.

The arrival of a heavy snowfall meant one thing. Action at the sand pit. Nowadays when I look back, I visualise a place of 'Winter Olympic' proportions. In reality it was a largish circular cavity in the corner of the field adjacent to the local water tower.

It was a happy gathering place and in the winter months we turned it into our own Cresta Run. Garden sheds and garages were raided for toboggans, tea trays and anything else that would slip successfully over the ground.

Our preliminary runs were all about preparing the terrain. Large clumps of thistles had to be scythed down and holes filled in. Slowly but surely we began to work up a good head of steam.

And then problems began.

Picture the rim of a crater, crowded with bodies all the way round being launched simultaneously downwards. Complete mayhem often resulted at the bottom with missiles seemingly coming at you from all angles. A successful run came not from being the fastest, but from having good anticipatory powers in avoiding the three Parker brothers, of farming stock, heading for you at breakneck speed on an old car bonnet, or from my big brother who echoed, "Look out, I'm on me way!" as he launched himself on the biggest and fastest sledge around.

At quieter moments my sisters and their girl friends would slide genteelly down the sand pit. Even some parents ventured over the fields to steal a bit of the action when their busy lives allowed it and if not too many of the more raucous lads were around to ridicule them.

*

"What! Writing name in the snow with pee will make yer willy stick in the ice?"

"Yes, Ken. One of the big lads told me last week. Must be true, so watch it."

"Fiddlesticks. Anyway I'm desperate and not goin' home to do it."

A fall of snow both covered up and revealed at the same time. I was fascinated by the delicate, almost filigree-like tracks left by foxes, stoat, rabbits, pheasant and other wild animals. Man, by comparison left large, uncontrolled, intrusive clodhopper imprints.

It was a clear sign to me who were the outsiders, the visitors to the countryside.

Winter steadily dragged itself forward.

Christmas time brought excursions across the fields in search of holly trees, mistletoe and fir cones. My father always insisted on a proper holly tree to erect in our front room.

A proper, very prickly, free holly tree.

"And try and find one with berries on," came the final order before we departed for the woods.

126

Later, we did manage to get, or should I say were offered, fir trees. Trees that had been stolen in the dead of the night from Delamere Forest and subsequently confiscated by the police.

It was no coincidence that Uncle Jim was a member of the force.

We had plenty of enjoyable times but did tire of the short days, the dark evenings meaning an early return to barracks at least for me and my siblings.

I don't recall too many winters that were very severe, apart from 1947 when I had to strain on tiptoe in order to see the neighbours' house after we had made a path through the snow from the road to the front door.

It was not until Easter was on the horizon that we felt we could start emerging from our cocoons.

"The days are stretching out," Mother optimistically kept telling us, more I suspect to bolster her own spirits, knowing that soon her squabbling offsprings would no longer be constantly under her feet in the restricted confines of the house.

*

The arrival of Spring to the countryside was a sublime experience. My favourite time of year. And still is.

We drift into the other seasons, but not Spring. Its arrival has a profound effect upon the body chemistry. It's acute, it arrives and you know it.

As a youngster, expectations were unlimited. Wild dreams had no boundaries.

It was a time, and still is a time, when I can forget the unpalatable, the disappointments.

A time to start afresh. To change the way of doing things. A clear, uncluttered road ahead, at least for a while until reality catches up with me.

If I was the Minister of Time, I would have Spring heralding in the new year and ditch dreary January for good.

Leaving behind the smoky, open fires of the house and sucking in that new, Spring air was so memorable, even for rather insensitive schoolboys.

Something was afoot.

In the fields, it was fascinating to see the ruddy-faced farmers straddling their beasts of battle, powerful Fordson Major tractors, turning over the soil ready for sowing. The noisy seagulls winging overhead looked for any morsels that were being churned up.

Often the farmers used a limestone mixture called marl to reduce acidity and a common ingredient was bits of broken clay pipes. Ted Littler in his role as a romantic archaeologist didn't agree.

"Naaw, rubbish. It's them old farmers over centuries ago discarding their fragile clay pipes when done with. Broke easily and rare they are. Look at 'em markings. Worth collecting you know."

Eventually he was put right by a farmer who told him he bought lorry loads of reject material off the local clay works. Rare they weren't but it didn't stop loads of them being stockpiled by Ted and my brother, trying diligently to match up pieces to make a complete pipe.

Keen gardeners manhandling their mowers for the first cut of the year added to the heady elixir with the smell of newly-cut grass.

As is so often said – "If you could have bottled it, you'd have made a million".

All around the countryside newness was emerging. Bulbs, having languished in the cold, damp earth for months, began to add their contribution. Great swathes of bluebells and celandines erupted into full colour, presenting a wonderful effect in one of our favourite woods near to the bypass road.

We literally grew up with this wood as it had been severely cut down by Italian prisoners soon after the end of World War II – presumably for some good reason, but I never found out why.

Old man Crofty and railwayman Johnson's immaculately-kept, prissy gardens further down the road started to produce results after endless hours spent manicuring their small front patches. Their tulips and daffodils appeared on cue.

The concept of garden centres was not even at the embryonic stage and rarely did anyone spend money on plants, apart from parting with a few coppers at Woolworths on lettuce and cress seeds, peas and beans.

Splitting roots, taking cuttings and swopping plants was the order of the day.

No fancy peat-free material or John Innes products.

Armed with shovel and wheelbarrow, many of the grown-ups raced to scoop up the latest droppings, still steaming, from the horse-drawn delivery vehicles that plied their trade up and down the lane.

"I saw it first," was often heard, but as for most things in life it was a question of first come, first served. Most of it found its way around the base of highly prized rose bushes.

Along the verges and in the gardens such as ours, where nature moved on undisturbed by man, primroses and cowslips began opening up, colouring the landscape like an artist's palette.

The elm, beech and oaks, rising majestically like brooding guardians amongst the miles of hawthorn and blackberry hedging along the lane and fields, began to lose their skeletal silhouettes as the first buds burst forth.

And if further proof was needed to confirm the arrival of Spring you only had to cock your ear out of the window as day was breaking – not that I was regular at such a practice, unless I was making an early start to see my heroes on the race track at Oulton Park.

The blackbird generally got the singing off to an early start, galvanising many of the other common birds such as song thrush, wood-pigeon, robin, wren and doves into action.

Occasionally my brother reckoned he could detect the more rare pheasant and warblers in the wood across the lane from our house.

But then he would, wouldn't he? Being older, more knowledgeable and the local ornithological expert!

So he said.

And of course he always laid claim to hearing the first cuckoo, a truly scientific signal that Spring had arrived. It was pointless arguing with him.

Bird song at Spring time is about establishing territory: the 'get off my patch, I was here first' approach. It is the prelude to pairing-up, nest building, laying eggs, incubating and raising young.

Flocks of lapwings increasingly made their presence felt over the ploughed fields, wheeling to and fro and then suddenly descending, sliding sideways en masse towards the ground like falling leaves. It was their way of defending their nesting sites from predators, particularly the carrion crows lurking in tall trees nearby.

Later in the day, skylarks would fill the air with their sustained warbling, often non-stop for minutes on end, as they hovered almost out of sight.

Who am I to argue with Shelley's 'To a skylark' where he describes the bird as 'showering the earth with a rain of melody.' It took something special to impress a bunch of young lads that life couldn't get much better.

Strangely, the free-spirited skylarks managed it.

It was also a time that toads and frogs started to get down to business. With my mates it was off to trawl ponds and water-filled ditches for spawn. It became almost accepted practice that we country 'bumpkins' would take Kilner jars, with my mother's approval, filled with spawn to school for the teacher to explain to the 'townies' a bit about procreation.

It never occurred to me at the time but it was probably considered by the teacher as the first attempt at explaining the facts of life to children. It fascinated all the class to see a small insignificant black blob, surrounded by jelly, begin to elongate, grow a head and tail and then sprout legs in a matter of days.

At some stage they must have been returned to nature by the teacher, into the nearest pool of water or the local canal that ran through Chester.

Or, more likely, down the school drain?

*

"Let's go bird nesting." Sounds harmless enough.

It was a common cry amongst my mates at this time of the year when bird activity was reaching its zenith. What we really meant was, "Let's look for birds' nests, let's see how many eggs there are and take some out."

I admit to struggling how best to describe as an adult what I did as a child. After all, I have been leading you on, telling you of our wonderful empathy with nature in Guilden Sutton. Respecters of the countryside and all that.

Let me get the bad side out straight away. OK, we were guilty of collecting birds' eggs. But it didn't feel like a crime then and in fact it wasn't an illegal pastime.

We felt that we approached all nests with a real sense of responsibility. Honestly.

Of course part of the exercise was one of curiosity, finding out the kind of bird, whether it had started to lay, and if so how many eggs. In our defence, the majority of birds around the village were prolific egg-layers, producing at least five and the tits and water birds, such as moorhens and coots, often went well into double figures.

So there was an element of only taking a relatively small proportion from each nest, knowing that often at least four or five would be laid as replacements.

Normally the person who found a nest would claim, using the local lingo, the 'fog egg', and the 'sec egg' went to the next in line.

We generally left it at that, but I have no doubts that some of my mates occasionally revisited to add to their collections.

The position and construction of nests told me much about the birds themselves. At the basic level, the tawny owl appeared a lazy creature, laying directly in a tree hole with no attempt at making a nest. A small scrape in a field that often was hard to detect was the nest of the lapwing.

Blackbirds and thrushes exhibited far more building skills, constructing very robust cup-shaped nests in hedges and low trees, from dried grass and dead leaves, completed with a lining of mud. Master plasterers indeed. Curiously the blackbird but not the thrush added a further lining of grass, presumably for a bit of luxury during sitting time,

Untidy piles of sticks at the tops of large trees told me that the bad old rooks and carrion crows had hit town. They worked on the principle that if you threw together enough building material, sooner or later a few would actually jam and stay where they were placed. I never saw a nest dislodged, even after the most severe of gales.

And they were very safe from the probing hands of young boys.

None of my gang of mates ever managed to peer into a rook's nest. The well-developed communal life of rooks led to dense estate-style living, accompanied by a constant, chattering raucous din. The following year, a brisk rebuilding job and the rooks were back in residence.

By far the hardest workers were the tits and wrens who beavered away, spending hours and hundreds of journeys transporting moss, leaves, grass and fine feathers to make the cosiest of nests to keep the elements at bay.

And the swallow could lay claim to being the most inventive.

"Look at that. Clever blighter, using that rusty old nail projecting from the wall of a barn to prop his nest on," my brother remarked, impressing us with more of his nature trivia.

We often watched them at work on Dandy's farm, where we bought our potatoes, painstakingly building up their nests from pellets made with airborne stems of grass, mixed with mud. Engineering geniuses.

Many families down the lane kept birds of some description. We had a couple of pigeon fanciers, who regularly parcelled their beloved birds up in wickerwork baskets, strapped them precariously across the back of their rickety old bikes, and headed unsteadily off in the failing light to Mickle Trafford station, some two miles away.

Propping their bikes up by the milk churns and red buckets of sand on the platform they'd search for the porter. Invariably he'd be found snoozing alongside his scrawny cat in the shadows cast by a line of oil lamps.

"Be sure they are well secured in the goods wagon," they added, waving them goodbye for their journey that could be up to 200 miles or so, often down through Shropshire, Herefordshire and further south.

Released by a friendly porter and helped by a prevailing tail wind, good navigational skills and a bit of luck, I dare say, we would see them return to their lofts next day, seemingly none the worse for wear for what I thought was a rather pointless exercise.

Our birds were a bit less mobile.

"Isn't it about time we had some more day-old chicks from Evans's farm?" regularly sighed Jean, my younger sister with obvious latent maternal enthusiasm.

Their home for about a month was a straw-filled cardboard box, squeezed into the small hearth close to the open fire in our living room. It was hard to imagine that these same small loveable, yellow balls of fluff could in a matter of weeks become arrogant, strutting adults that thought nothing about attacking our feeding hands.

The excitement of the daily 'hide and seek' game, searching for their eggs, made it all worthwhile.

That was until Christmas arrived.

There was little philanthropic about my dad. The Rhode Island Reds were, in his eyes, an investment.

"Sorry kids, one of your chickens will have to go."

That was the signal for farm labourer Parker to come around.

"This the one for the pot, eh, Mr Wi'brum?" he queried, roughly grabbing the unfortunate candidate. A sharp tug of the neck, silence and it was over to my parents to begin the laborious job of preparing the bird for the oven.

Pulling with pliers, singeing with a blowlamp, removing entrails.

Today the same objective is achieved by opening a plastic bag grabbed from a supermarket shelf.

"No, not Perky!" we all cried.

Sadly our favourite cockerel had had the short straw drawn for him. It was too much for us to bear. That year is remembered more for tears than cheers.

Half-eaten meals were left as we sloped away from the table to our bedrooms.

Some years later when the chickens were a distant memory, I recall my brother cobbling together a makeshift aviary out of the remains of the hen run to house a couple of owls that he had found injured whilst out on one of his many nature rambles.

For a time there was harmony, but it was short-lived as we discovered that the tawny owl was now sharing the enclosure with a pile of feathers.

"Poor barn owl," said Mother consoling her eldest son, when she heard the news. Shortly after, the tawny owl was given its freedom, presumably feeling much better after proving that cannibalism was alive and well in the animal kingdom.

*

Wimbledon Fortnight.

To us it meant strawberries, not tennis.

It was time for our annual pilgrimage to Farndon, a small village on the banks of the River Dee a few miles south of Chester. It was the only source of strawberries for miles around and the season lasted little longer than the action on the grass courts in SW19.

The rarity value in those days elevated the fruit almost to a cult level.

Later my mother would reflect, "Well maybe you can buy them now in these fancy new supermarkets all year round, but they don't taste anything like real strawberries."

I agreed with her that I too, didn't care much for the enormous, tasteless heart-shaped fruit, which arrived daily by the planeload from the sunny climes of the world.

"Give me Farndon strawberries any day," she would add when in pensive mood.

*

"D'you reckon it will be warm enough to swim in yet?"

"What?" queried my mate Jack.

"The Gowy, of course," I snapped back.

"Oh yer, could give it a whirl this weekend, eh. Hope it is."

Soon after lunchtime, Jack turned up and told me he had a puncture so could I give a 'crossie' on my bike down to the river. Giving a lift on the crossbar sounds risky but the worst that ever happened was scraped knees and elbows if we fell off.

Turning off the twisty main road through the village it was all downhill along a track that was often used by gypsies who passed through from time to time.

The popular area to swim was near the Oxen bridge close to where the Milton Brook from Barrow joined the River Gowy. Already there was plenty of action in the water.

"Hi lads, hurry up, it's great in!"

It took some believing when I studied their grimaces and blue tinges of their extremities. But saving face was the name of the game. Once one had gone in, no one dared not to.

We ditched our bike by the others near to the bridge and within seconds were ready for action. Invariably it was freezing, but keeping on the move eased the enforced pain.

Jumping off the bridge, a popular activity, was fraught with danger.

"Make sure you get to the deep bit," was advice freely given from down below. Failure and it was a short, painful and ignominious struggle through the bulrushes to the sanctuary of the river bank.

I limped for months after I failed this test one particular summer. But like a fool I went back for more.

Stretched out along the sloping bank of the river on our towels in the deep grass, we absorbed the blazing sun, bringing normality back to our cold but refreshed bodies.

Time to indulge in fantasy thoughts.

As quietness descended and the river was once again a tranquil place, swans casually drifted by on the current whilst heron fell back into their military poses a safe distance away, looking for that elusive tiddler.

Cows, rudely pushed away by our spirited arrival, nervously eased themselves back to the muddy water's edge.

We would put off the uphill journey home till we could no longer ignore our hunger pangs. Slowly we regrouped and headed back. Often we would walk all the way, not bothering to use our bikes.

Time had temporarily been forgotten. As the local sage Ted Littler reminded me many years later, "Ken, that walk back from the Gowy was always special."

He went on, "They were long, poetic, quintessential English evenings, strolling along familiar tracks and hedgerows as the sun began to settle over the distant Welsh Hills."

A poet laureate waiting in the wings was our Ted.
Our bodies and minds felt the benefit of that brief sabbatical.

Chapter 17

Hooked on water

For 'pond' read 'pit'. For 'pit' read 'pond'.

I never fathomed out our inconsistency in differentiating the two.

Maybe a pit was synonymous with smelly, stagnant water whilst ponds were cleaner and had an air of superiority with bigger fish, larger nests and taller bulrushes.

But whatever, I found them all irresistible. And so did my mates.

Around the village we had perhaps about a dozen that were on our visiting list. There was something magical, almost magnetic-like that sucked us towards them. These relatively small splashes of water had their own very distinctive character, unique charm and were constantly changing throughout the seasons.

There is a certain logic in mentioning 'the old pond' for starters. It was closest to my house and although it supported little in the way of interesting animal life it was the first bit of water that most of us cut our teeth on, or fell into off the rope as we bravely attempted to swing across it.

It stank most of the time, was covered with large overhanging unfriendly brambles and I don't recall any of us ever catching even a tiddler in the murky, stagnant water. Not even semi-professional fisherman Crofty had success here.

But it whetted my appetite for the intricacies of pond life.

Bailey's pit, on the south side of the railway track to the rear of my house was a favourite amongst the keener anglers. Good-sized roach and rudd, and enormous eels lurking in the dominating thick swathes of rushes and reeds, were the main attraction.

"So who was really to blame?" asked my eternally patient mother, as we sat in the casualty department of Chester Royal Infirmary.

"Did you do it yourself or was it one of those naughty friends of yours that managed to get the hook firmly embedded into your hand?" she went on.

"Just happened, Mum. Honest," was my reply.

Another imperfect end to a near-perfect day at a pit.

It had the added dubious interest of nestling up against pig sties which constantly oozed an obnoxious whiff and scoffing noises day and night. I always felt that there was a certain amount of secrecy surrounding the goings-on at Bailey's farm. Struggling to stay upright, rusty, corrugated iron sheeting conjured up a place under siege.

Like, come so far up the cindered track to the farm but no further.

To be fair to farmer Bailey, he was a kindly old bloke, never without his flat hat tilted heavily over to one side and clothing that had stiffened as the result of years of intimate contact with pig swill. He must have needed heavy lifting tackle to extricate himself from this straitjacket at the end of a day at 'the office.'

Touring the area in his modern, dark blue Foden flat-backed lorry, he regularly returned laden with umpteen bins filled with swill from local schools, hospitals and army depots. Cutlery, smashed crockery, watches and pencils were natural bed partners with potato peelings and other rejected tasty morsels that smelt to high heaven.

Where would we have been without these kings of the recycling world?

What little the pigs left behind, the marauding chickens hoovered up at their leisure. Farmer Bailey never shooed us away from his pond and we considered him a good egg but a bit of a recluse.

*

The Stile field pond was our favourite – a good size, a handful of bushes that gave sanctuary to birds and small muddy mini-islands created by cows were dotted around the edge.

"Where you off fishin' now, Jack or Tony or Dave or Uncle Tom Cobbleigh and all?"

"Stile field of course," was the reply almost without exception.

It must have been a good pond because we had a fair hike to get there. Four fields at least and two railway lines if my memory serves me right.

It was where I baptised my new rod.

"Where d'you get that one from, Ken?" asked Jack.

"Bought the cane last week at Woollies. Twelve-footer. Just got some new ones in. Had to walk all the way home 'cos the bus conductor thought it too big to get on.

"Could have hit him 'cos it was raining as well," I carried on.

Converting the cane into a fishing rod was a relatively easy operation. Four or five circular pieces of thin wire were bound onto the rod at about two foot intervals, with one at the tip. Typewriter ribbon spools, suitably converted with a Meccano nut and bolt for the handle, proved excellent reels, around which I wound very thin catgut. The float was a cork, drilled to take a quill from a large bird's feather, with a blob of red paint to tell me when the fish were biting.

To complete this state-of-the-art equipment, a pin, bent into a simple hook, was attached to the end of the gut.

A couple slices of bread and I was ready to amuse myself for hours on end.

None of us had proper rods and could only dream about them.

*

And then one day we witnessed something that none of us present would forget.

There he was, sitting on the edge of our pond, surrounded by all the latest paraphernalia you could imagine. Tons of the latest gear.

This old bloke.

Well, at least as old as my oldest teacher at a rough guess and that was old. What was this stranger doing at our pond? My pond.

A slight movement of his head was an acknowledgement of our arrival at the pond side.

Our preparation time was seconds before we made our first casts. Again it was only seconds before roach and rudd were queueing up for a tasty meal of stale bread. Bite after bite, they kept coming, filling our jam jars as if there was no tomorrow.

Not just me but all my mates were pulling them out as fast as we could. The old man kept casting, looking intent, lifting his float now and again. Still no fish, not even a bite.

"What's he doin'?" Jack quietly whispered into my ear.

"Dunno," I replied.

"He's no idea," said Dave as he crawled around from the far bank, almost falling into the water with amusement. It was beginning to get through to the old man that he was becoming the centre of attention and I'm not sure he was enjoying it.

How would he take it? I thought.

He was big enough to give us all a good clip around the ears. Our parents would have said "serve you right for being impudent". But we wouldn't have told our parents for fear of getting further punishment for cheek to older people.

Then he got up from his canvas seat, stretched himself and slowly walked around the edge of the pond towards us where we had all gathered to watch the comedy show that he had been performing for us.

"Hello lads," he said.

His large shadow hung over us on the grass bank.

We mumbled hellos back.

"Biting well today, eh," he continued.

"Err, yep. Not bad. Seem to like bread in this pond."

"Is that so?" he replied. "I only brought maggots and got my hook down near the bottom."

"Well that's your problem,' said Jack. "Should be no deeper than eighteen inches, that's where you'll catch 'em."

The man coughed slightly, "I'm, err, going pike fishing tomorrow with my club and need some live bait for the day. D'you think that..?"

He almost got bowled over with the response. To a lad we all spluttered, "I'll catch you some, Mister."

So we all went home happy. The pike angler no doubt told his mates that he had a very successful day at a local pond, getting the live bait. We laughed ourselves silly all the way home at his expense.

The lesson we all learnt that day?

"Success doesn't come with what you've got. It's what you do with what you've got."

My dad was impressed when I related the story to him and my son Tim often recites the modern equivalent;

"He's got all the gear, but little idea."

*

Ever heard of a thinking man's pit? We had one.

Near to the water tower. It was not everyone's cup of tea and was only for the intrepid, those who wanted temporary solace, to 'get away from it all.'

It was getting a little too close for comfort to Hoole Hall where a particularly irritable and unfriendly farmer held court. We occasionally saw him riding on fox hunts. He fitted Oscar Wilde's observation wonderfully – "the English country gentleman galloping after a fox: the unspeakable in full pursuit of the uneatable."

It was in no man's land. A long way from home, should we encounter trouble.

I always felt that the intimidating wood immediately to the west of the pit, filled with tall congested, straggly trees, gave the area a feeling of foreboding. A stygian gloom constantly hung over the area, even on the sunniest of days.

From a distance it beckoned to us.

"Come over and visit me, but be prepared for the unexpected," it seemed to hint.

It was without noise. That was eerie. It could have been home to a long-lost tribe for all we knew.

I never ventured into its heart. Neither did my mates.

The large, tall, sentinel-style, rusting square water tank, resting precariously on ivy clad, crumbling brick pillars at the edge of the trees, could have doubled up as a watchtower.

It took little of my imagination to make out the farmer and his ruddy-faced labourers, appearing over the top ledge armed with their double-barrelled shotguns at the ready, just as we were on the verge of removing eggs from a moorhen's nest, which were dotted around the reed beds.

It was a piece of nature from another age, probably undisturbed for hundreds of years, apart from the occasional sortie by the local lads. Certainly far too spooky for the girls in the village to entertain, provoking our chant,

"Scaredy-cats, scaredy-cats, sitting on the door mat."

Undisturbed for aeons, we looked in awe at the predator-like silvery-scaled custodians of the deep water, moving round in a menacing convoy.

Truly dinosaurial in size.

Truly fisherman's language was in order.

Reference books couldn't cope.

"And yer twelve-inch wooden school ruler won't be long enough," added a smart lad.

"Even if you have the strength to land one," added another.

I never fished the water tower pond. I went to experience the past and leave it untouched, apart from the odd egg or two.

Swallows were regular visitors. They were good company and made us feel a bit more comfortable. No doubt they were attracted by banquet proportions of flies swarming in dark uncontrollable, billowing clouds above the pond.

"Surely they crash sometime in their lives?" I often thought.

But no.

These high-speed fork-tailed flying aces raked the skies for food.

Never putting a foot wrong or a wing, they performed an aerial ballet for us every time we visited, to perfection.

Mealtime completed, they would return to their 'wattle and daub' housing community in the nooks and crannies of the water tower.

Twilight came prematurely to this secluded and special ecosystem of ours and occasionally, if we were brave enough to stay a while, we witnessed barn owls preparing for the night with a few yawns, blinks and wing stretching prior to setting off in search of mice and rats.

A clandestine wood and equally clandestine nocturnal operator in complete harmony.

"Nature doesn't come much rawer," I often thought.

It wasn't a place to hang around when the gloom was gathering so we were smartly into our stride to cross a few fields before picking up the welcoming gas lights of the main lane that ran by our houses.

I hope the farmer and his successors have left this special piece of natural history alone and not seen fit, God forbid, to turn it into a garden centre or theme park.

The fear of great loss and sadness prevents my returning, should changes have been made.

*

All our ponds had a particular role to play in the busy, inquisitive lives that we led. Those without vegetation looked bare and soulless. Nowhere for bird nesting – but ideal for sailing our boats on. Easy to launch and no reeds to get in the way or clog the propellers.

Sails, elastic bands, jetex propellants and small diesel engines were used depending upon our circumstances and ingenuity.

If swans happened to take out a mortgage on a pond, and they were regulars at particular sites, we stayed clear.

"You know they are capable of breaking young lads' arms with their wings," busybody neighbours kept reminding me, but as far as I know it's never happened on this island of ours to even the stupidest of lads.

We didn't argue with the kings of the bird world and generally kept a hedge between us and them, particularly during breeding.

Mallard, heron, coots and moorhens settled on many ponds, no doubt encouraged by the farmers who found them useful for gracing the dinner table when expecting relatives and friends for the week-end.

Small, shallow ponds gave me the opportunity to investigate pond life at close quarters. Stretched out on our bellies, sleeves rolled well up past our elbows, we got a close-up of water-flea, mayfly, stickle-back, pond skaters and stick insects in action.

The star of the show for me was the inventive caddis fly who could make a pupating chamber, its house to you and me, out of sand grains, twigs, and leaf fragments.

Could it be that the modest caddis fly larva gave me some of the best advice of my life?

That most things can be achieved given time, patience and only the most basic of building blocks.

Chapter 18

Never quite finished

We all knew who she was talking about.

"Left to him, none of you lot would ever have been finished properly."

How true my mother's words were when she occasionally gave vent to her anarchic sense of humour.

Words that were echoed by friends and relatives alike.

"That dad of yours. Couldn't finish a job to save his life," added Aunt Sal in one of her many vitriolic moments.

A wonderful childhood vision of a fishpond is still with me, even though then I was barely out of my nappies. To be fed with a small stream flowing down a beautifully manicured rockery. It was a long time, a very long time in the planning stage. Dad led the discussions, always telling us what we really wanted.

Designing and redesigning ad nauseum.

The hard work had been done. We'd beavered away with our bloodied hands and kid-sized tools, sculpturing a large hollow out of the ground at the far end of the lawn.

Boulders small and large had been accumulated by the four of us on various sorties to the seaside, quarries and just trawling the ditches of the neighbourhood.

Father always had a thousand and one reasons to delay.

"In the spring, eh, kids? That's a good time. Warmer then."

"All right Dad. Promise?"

Spring came. And spring went.

"Must just finish the kitchen first, eh kids? Got to keep on right side of Mother."

Gnawing away in his mind was another extension on the extension that he was nearly finishing at the end of garage.

"But Dad, can't we do it ourselves? We know what to do."

"Right son, but, but not quite yet."

And so it went on.

Slowly leaving the embryonic stage, boulder by boulder, brick by brick, stone by stone, things started to happen. We constantly had to wait for materials.

"Got some cement coming next week from Joe Wotchamacallit. And how about you lads getting busy with barrow to replenish gravel stock with more from road outside?"

Sheepishly, we did sorties when dusk had arrived so prying eyes didn't see us and saved us embarrassment. Father was comfortable doing it in full daylight.

Little did our local council realise that gradually we were removing parts of the road running past the house for constructing garden paths, footings for walls and so on.

"Saving 'em a job, eh? Would only block drains if we didn't sweep 'em up," argued Father very convincingly, to himself.

Suffice to say, the pond never did see water and was soon lost under accumulating debris and whatever else Father brought back to Number 40.

A rockery of sorts eventually emerged, more by default, as wild flowers, in spite of Father, started to establish themselves on the pile of boulders that had lain for years waiting, just waiting to be lovingly placed closer together in a designed fashion.

I exorcised this particular burden from my mind when I recently made a pond that Father would have been proud of, but he wouldn't have approved of my buying plastic lining, pebbles and fancy plants to adorn the surrounding soil.

"If you'd told me earlier, son, I'd have found some in shed or up garden for you," he no doubt is saying to me, from, hopefully above the clouds. If you believe that sort of thing.

It takes little of my imagination to picture the present owners of my parents' house calling in eminent professors of archaeology, pronouncing on whether recently exposed artefacts lying in a circular fashion were part of ritualistic remains dating back to the Stone Age or earlier.

I would soon dampen their enthusiasm by telling them they're circa 1948 and intended to be used for goldfish.

*

Our back garden wall was a regular talking-point up and down the lane. My dad took almost as long to build it as that one in China that's a bit more famous.

It ran along the west side of the lawn and I can assure you that no two pieces of material used were the same. Cunningly, it was of dry-wall construction. Not that my father was attempting to mimic craftsmen over the ages that developed this highly skilled approach of placing stones and the like together, forming robust structures, without the need for mortar.

Oh no. Dad's reason was far more practical.

The bricks were laid dry so that should another job come along that needed a brick or two, or stones, then his wall simply became his supply stockpile.

So the wall height and length simply ebbed and flowed, sometimes maybe as high as five feet. Then the following week down to eighteen inches and then we could throw insults once again at the Parker lads next door. Winds and the high spirits of those lads occasionally made for some unsightly bulges that Father constantly spent time putting right.

How Mother never found one of us trapped, or worse, under Father's attempt at fortifying the back garden, I'll never know.

Our neighbours had the not-so-bright idea at the time of planting a privet hedge to bring about a bit more permanency to the dividing line. Against all odds, it did eventually emerge above Father's wall. That signalled the end of the need for Father's love and joy and his 'stock' was quickly deployed in many and varied ways around his 'estate'.

*

Inside the house, life could be equally precarious from 'things', hanging around,

"Leave 'em be. I'll want 'em again next week. They're not in the way."

"Well, maybe not in yours, Charlie, but in everyone else's," Mother regularly muttered to herself. Raising her voice would have made precious little difference. They would eventually find another resting place, just as inconvenient as the first.

"Putting and taking," we grew to know it.

Painting progressed to the undercoat stage and never further. Finishing coats weren't in his vocabulary.

"I might want to change it, lad, and that'll be a waste of paint won't it?"

Nails protruded.

"Why not knock 'em all the way in, Dad?"

"Never know when you might want to pull 'em out again if something goes wrong."

And he patented the idea of using screws, doubling up as drawer and door handles, until he had time to make the proper thing. He measured time in years not days.

Snagging of clothes and broken fingernails were par for the course in Number 40.

Ironically, another danger lay in an area that Father should have known better.

Wiring. Electrical wiring.

Here was man that had spent years educating himself, going to Liverpool Technical College four nights a week, eventually qualifying as a chartered Electrical Engineer and who took up lecturing the subject to enthusiastic students.

He was forever chasing yet another wire up the wall, belting hell out of the brickwork with his bolster chisel and lump hammer. Straggling wire ends sprouted up anywhere and everywhere over the house.

"You'll be thankful for the extra light, when I'm done," he sharply rebuked any comments coming from us.

Mother's meek, "try and keep the dust down dear," was drowned by another ear-splitting noise reverberating through the house.

And to this day I can still see the look on visitors' faces when they were confronted in the entrance hall with an industrial-style panel housing ten switches, all without any indication of what did what and to where.

It often seemed like minutes before visitors managed to get the right light to pay a visit to the loo upstairs. Even Mother was still struggling with what switched what on, after 30 years of practice and more.

The same arrangement gave us kids fun and games upstairs, with bedroom lights rudely awakening somnolent bodies.

Back at the combined control and fuse box high up in the back kitchen, perpetually covered with a fine covering of dust laden cobwebs, further mayhem existed. Redundant boxes and switches were left in-situ.

"Just in case, m'lad. Never know when you need a spare. And those damn lads that came round the other day from the electricity board. Going on about safety and the like. I told 'em I teach the subject. That silenced 'em and they left sharply. Cheeky young upstarts."

"Yes, Dad, no Dad. You carry on in your own sweet way," I often thought.

What do they say – "like father like son"?

Mmmm, perhaps nowadays I should listen to my children a little more.

*

Excitement was mounting in the household. Our 'well to do' relatives who had emigrated to Vancouver were due to land anytime now in Liverpool on the *Empress of Canada*.

Dad's eldest sister, Rose, had married a purser who worked on the ships that sailed up to Alaska. And now, with their teenage daughters, they were heading back for Chester in their brand new Standard Vanguard which they'd picked up from the docks.

Father thought to himself, "Serving hatch! That's it. About time I made a serving hatch in the wall between the kitchen and the dining room."

After all he'd only had at least fifteen years to carry out another of his many longterm projects and he thought now a good time to do it.

He set to, smashing a fair-sized hole in the wall, whilst Mother had gone to Chester, doing last-minute shopping, getting what she could to feed extra mouths for several days – and on ration books, which our rich Canadian relatives didn't have to endure and which caused more than a little ill-feeling with Mother.

Although dusting was pretty low down on her priority list, it was obvious, even to a ten-year-old lad, that she was attempting to apply a little gloss to what can best be described as an honest-to-goodness working homestead.

Dropping her multitude of shopping bags on the doorstep and struggling with the front door, she could just make out her husband's silhouette, moving round as if in a Saharan desert storm.

It was one of those memorable moments fixed firmly in the minds of those present. The king of the castle was instantly dethroned without Mother even uttering a word. Eye-to-eye contact was all that was needed. Fortunately my father's dad happened to be there, and had a friendly chat to his eldest son, pointing out that what he'd done was perhaps not very sensible!

Talk about someone with his tail between his legs.

Now Father was furtively looking round, attempting to redo the jigsaw that he'd spread out before himself on the floor, the table and kitchen slab. Slowly he made some sense of the jagged edged bits and applied a rough plaster coat, all the time whistling 'Pack up Your Troubles in Your Old Kitbag', to hide a rare moment of embarrassment. A quick coat of whitewash and the strategic hanging of a picture brought that little episode to an end.

Aunt Rose and her family duly arrived, 'did Europe' in their car and eventually disappeared back across the Atlantic. Father's pipe dream remained just that and the wall was never breached again.

Serving hatches had obviously gone out of fashion.

*

Our school homework, however, was a completely different kettle of fish. That did receive his undivided attention and we couldn't go up the wooden hills to bed until Father had checked and ensured that at least his kids finished things.

Also from Léonie Press:

MEMORIES OF A CHESHIRE CHILDHOOD - MEMORIAL EDITION
Lenna Bickerton (ISBN 1 901253 00 7)

Lenna describes life in Northwich around the First World War through the sharp senses of a child. Her memories are vivid: duck eggs for breakfast, dancing to Grandad's gramophone, a near tragedy at a watermill, her schooldays, the sights and sounds of the old town, the smells of wild flowers, busy boat traffic on the canal — and the menacing "Ginny Greenteeth." This memorial edition includes her obituary. **£4.99**

NELLIE'S STORY – *A Life of Service*
Elizabeth Ellen Osborne (ISBN 1 901253 15 5)

Elizabeth Ellen Osborne was born at Shipbrook, near Northwich, Cheshire, in 1914. Her father was a farm worker and the family lived in a tied cottage. When she left school at 14 she went into service for the local 'toffs'. Following her marriage she was a nurse, a 'dinner lady' and a much-loved foster mother. As a Royal British Legion welfare officer she rode round Mid-Cheshire on a 90cc motorcycle until she was 80. **£5.99**

DIESEL TAFF – *From 'The Barracks' to Tripoli*
Austin Hughes (ISBN 1 901253 14 7)

Austin Hughes was born in February 1922 at 'The Barracks', a group of flea-ridden cottages deep in rural North Wales. From childhood he had loved heavy machinery and he learned to drive trucks and bulldozers. Then in 1940 he was called up to join the Royal Engineers. This was to be an experience which changed the young Welshman's life and earned him his nick-name 'Diesel Taff'. By the end of the war, he'd driven thousands of miles across deserts and mountains, transporting heavy plant, building roads and air strips, clearing avalanches and ferrying refugees. **£8.99**

HAPPY DAYS AND HEARTBREAK DAYS
A farmer's son relives his 1920s childhood
Victor William Dilworth (ISBN 1 901253 34 1)

A gem of rural English social history written through the innocent and curious eyes of a toddler and small boy, this book tells of the author's childhood on a Shropshire farm. Victor was the youngest of a large family, whose busy parents had little time for him until he could do some useful work. But he absorbed everything that was going on around him and asked endless questions. **£6.99**

PINAFORE STREET - A Fenland childhood
Kathleen Lord (ISBN 1 901253 39 2)

In vivid and witty detail, Kathleen Lord describes her childhood in Boston, Lincolnshire in the years after the First World War, bringing a long-gone era sharply into focus. Now nearly 90, her memoirs were written after she retired about 30 years ago and will be read with nostalgic pleasure by her contemporaries and with great interest by those who love social history. **£6.99**

Visit our website www.leoniepress.com to see our selection of books about Cheshire and other autobiographies.